Of Love and Death
Young Holocaust Survivors' Passage to Freedom

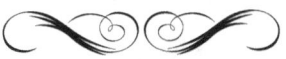

Miriam Segal Shnycer

AucTus Publishers

Copyright © 2019 Miriam Segal Shnycer
Book and cover design by Sarah Eldridge
Cover art and illustration by Angela Del Vecchio

Published by Auctus Publishers
606 Merion Avenue, First Floor
Havertown, PA 19083
Printed in the United States of America

All rights reserved. Scanning, uploading, and distribution of this book via the internet or via any other means without permission in writing from its publisher, Auctus Publishers, is illegal and punishable by law. Please purchase only authorized editions.

ISBN 978-1-7327882-1-3 (Electronic)
ISBN 978-1-7327882-0-6 (Softcover)

Praise for *Of Love and Death*

"Lessons learned from my mother and father: strength against all odds, standing tall in the face of hatred, and the courage to begin a new life and look to the future. As a child of Holocaust survivors, I am the result of my parents' strength, courage, and perseverance. The Holocaust was rarely spoken of during my childhood leaving missing pieces to my puzzle. Miriam Segal Shnycer, through her conversations and interviews, has been able to provide insight and to truthfully bring to life the impact the Holocaust left on my parents and in turn on my childhood. *Of Love and Death* completes the puzzle that was my childhood, the childhood of Holocaust survivors' children, and those left pondering how staying strong against all odds stands tall in the face of hatred."

—**Rosalie Lipshutz Swartz**, *daughter of Holocaust survivors Jozek and Hanka (Joseph and Ann Lipshutz)*

"*Of Love and Death: Young Holocaust Survivors' Passage to Freedom* vividly depicts the unfathomable horrors of the Holocaust. This incomparable saga shows us that people can overcome unspeakable adversities and hardships by calling on their innate resources of faith, courage, and perseverance. Every page of Shnycer's book underscores the triumphant resilience of the human spirit through its unforgettable characters who show us that love is always stronger than death. In clear, poetic prose, *Of Love and Death* relates the story of five people from three families who survived the Holocaust and went on to realize the American dream. The author's skillful and vibrant narration takes us to a place we've only read about in history books and makes this heartrending story about the Holocaust immediate and real for its readers. Shnycer brings all the characters to life so that we feel like we know each character intimately. The book's dialogue rings true with characters who never fail to touch our hearts and souls. I highly recommend this book for anyone desiring to learn the true story of the Holocaust. I will never forget the Lipschutz, Ferber, and Schnitzer families and how they prevailed over evil. They are an inspiration to all of us."

—**Catherine DePino, Ed.D**, *has written seventeen books about bullying, writing, and parenting. For many years, she worked as a teacher and department head in the Philadelphia School District and at Temple University as an adjunct assistant professor.*

"Miriam Segal Shnycer in her book, *Of Love and Death*, focuses on three families living in Krakow, Poland. We learn how individual family members dealt with the fear that came with the arrival of jackbooted-armed soldiers who sought to enslave the Jewish population. Later, the "Final Solution" called for the extermination of all the Jews. To survive, family members had to be smart, and they had to be brave. First person narratives of actual events take us from confronting Nazis on the streets, to false sanctuary across the Russian border, to the formation and later dissolution of the Jewish ghetto, to life in the obscene condition of the Plaszow concentration camp, to the miracle of Schindler's List and ultimately, to liberation. The author makes it clear that bravery was a key element of the ability to survive. But even more importantly, the characters, most of whom were her relatives, were able to survive because they were motivated by love and loyalty to each other. The author's account enables us to identify with real human beings. It is well-worth reading."

—**Gabriel J. Ferber**, *Child of Holocaust Survivors*

For my grandchildren
Eric Golberg, Cara Golberg, Ethan Silver, and Lindsey Silver
You light up my life

And
In Loving Memory of Members of the
Shnycer, Lipshutz, and Ferber families who perished in
the Holocaust

Foreword

Over seventy-three years ago, battle weary and exhausted young GI's truly glimpsed hell. Its gates were the portals to the Nazi concentration camps.

Among the lucky survivors to escape from the ashes were five members of three interrelated families. When Krakow, Poland was attacked by Germany on September 1, 1939, these survivors ranged in ages from three-years-old to twenty-years-old. In Miriam Segal Shnycer's beautifully written book, you will read about their astonishing journey from the ghetto, to the concentration camps, to the displaced persons camps, and to their finally coming to America.

The author is married to Wilus Schnitzer (William Shnycer) the youngest survivor. She introduces us to Jozek Lipschutz (Joseph Lipshutz) who would marry my cousin, Hanka Ferber (Ann Ferber). Jozek Lipschutz was fearless, a risk-taker with an insatiable desire to live.

I won't reveal the outcome of their extraordinary odyssey as told by the author, but I will say that a few family members and I survived because we had the good fortune to be on Schindler's List. While the world became deaf and blind, Oskar Schindler risked his life to save twelve hundred of his workers. Oskar Schindler was my angel.

I couldn't put this book down. The prisoners' tenacious will to live is in many cases what saved them.

The way we helped each other - one day at a time, one hour at a time.

I marvel at how Wilus Schnitzer, such a young child, who saw so much and suffered so much, was able to survive and build a wonderful life and family in the United States.

We are the eyewitnesses. In this book you will find the truth. We pass the torch of memory to all of you the future generations. Forgetting is dangerous.

Rena Finder, Schindler's List survivor and a narrator at the beginning of Steven Spielberg's *Schindler's List* DVD, is a member of Facing History and Ourselves. She speaks frequently about the Holocaust.

Author's Note

My husband, William Shnycer, and I dated as teenagers. I honored his wish not to ask him about his childhood spent in the Holocaust. He was able to compartmentalize, to keep his head clear for fitting into a new life. He studied English for a year and started his schooling for the first time in the ninth grade. He had much to look forward to and much to master.

After we married, and I had frequent conversations with members of the three connected families featured in my book, I was irresistibly drawn to their personal stories. Their history was full of love and death, courage and luck, and an indefatigable strength of will to survive.

My creative nonfiction book could not have been written without Joseph Lipshutz's brave introspection reliving this painful part of his life. I quickly realized in my interviews with him that I needed to include the Shnycer and Ferber families' stories. It was only after my husband retired that he agreed I could add his account to my book.

Although I dealt with broken memories, all of the events in my book are true. I was fortunate to know all the survivors. I can hear their voices in my head, visualize their expressions, and feel the depth of their feelings, all of which I have incorporated into their histories.

The survivors did not always recall every action and event in the same way or remember what another witness said. Where one family member recounted something and the other family member didn't remember it, I looked for collaborating information.

Rena Finder (Rena Ferber Finder), Schindler's List Holocaust survivor, and a narrator at the beginning of Steven Spielberg's *Schindler's List* DVD, is mentioned in the storytellers' narratives. Rena is a family member who provided valuable information. If she doubted something could have happened, and I had no other person aware of what took place, I did not include it in the book. I can't thank Rena enough for being so generous with her time and attention to detail.

Besides Rena, I owe a huge debt of gratitude to witnesses Victor (Viktor) and Regina Lewis, and Margot Schlesinger for their helpfulness. They all shared significant information and have enriched the telling of the storytellers' experiences.

Since my husband was very young when Germany invaded Krakow, Poland, I had to rely on the storytellers and the other witnesses to help relate parts of his early life.

Of Love and Death has five storytellers: Jozek Lipschutz (Joseph Lipshutz), Hanka Ferber (Ann Ferber), Roman Ferber, Frania Schnitzer, and Wilus Schintzer (William Shnycer). Each chapter identifies the character relating that part of the storytelling.

The book is separated into five sections: Prologue, Confinement, From Captivity to Liberation, After Liberation and Coming to America, and Epilogue. The dialogue, written in English, would have been spoken in Polish before they came to America.

What first propelled me to write this book is the event that took place when Russian soldiers confronted Jozek Lipshutz on a train. I was astonished by Jozek's risk-taking involving stealing maroon velvet material. You will find it in Chapter 6. His strength to do whatever it takes to stay alive occurs again and again in other chapters as Jozek uses his wits to combat the horrors of the Holocaust.

There's much I have learned from the accounts of these Holocaust witnesses. It's these individual chronicles that I have always found so compelling. The Holocaust survivors have important and unique stories to impart about their lives before the war, after Germany invades Poland, liberation, and beyond.

To my readers, I want to take you on a journey with these ordinary, spirited people who triumphed over evil, found a home in a new country, and captured the American dream.

"You gain strength, courage, and confidence by every experience in which you really stop to look fear in the face. You are able to say to yourself, 'I have lived through this horror. I can take the next thing that comes along.' You must do the things you think you cannot do."

-Eleanor Roosevelt

Cast of Characters

Lipschutz Family
Abraham: father, *Tatus*, deceased 1938 at age 55
Rosalia: mother, **Mamusia*, 50, homemaker
Milek: son, 22, attended university, works as an engineer in a metal shop
Jozek: son, 20, graduated high school, attended technical school, and works as a furrier
Sabcia: daughter, 17, seamstress for upscale dress shop
***Manek: son, 14, high school student

Ferber Family
Leon: father, *Tatus*, 44, successful salesman
****Malia: mother, **Mamusia*, 41, homemaker
***Manek: son, 17, university student
Hanka: daughter, 14, high school student
Roman: son, 6, bright child

Schnitzer Family
Henryk: father, *Tatus*, 32, owner of successful tailor shop
****Frania: mother, **Mamusia*, 30, homemaker
Wilus: son, 3, happy child

*Tatus, Polish word for father is used for father in the three families
**Mamusia, Polish word for mother is used for mother in the three families
***Lipschutz and Ferber families both have a son named Manek
****Malia Ferber and Frania Schnitzer are sisters

Prologue

January 25, 1945

      We walk in blinding swirling snow white as milk, two small phantasms. Huge snowdrifts blur our vision. Thin worn clothing our only protection against the frigid cold. We have no socks, no underwear. Our shoes are soaked. Our toes, fingers, and ears are numb. Wilus keeps sinking into the snow. I keep yanking him out. We trudge along until Auschwitz is in our sight. We have circled back.

Chapter 1

Explosions Burst in the Distance

Jozek

Friday, September 1, 1939, 5:30 a.m. The tranquil early morning quiet shatters at the thunderous roar of airplane engines.

I jump out of bed and yell to Milek, "It's the…"

"Luftwaffe," he interrupts. My brother springs out of his bed from under the window and pulls open the drapes. We stretch our necks skyward. My flimsy hope for peace has come to a devastating end.

Mamusia rushes into our makeshift bedroom in the dining room.

"Luftwaffe. Flying east," I hastily utter.

"It has come to this. Oh my G-d!" Mamusia exclaims. Planes overhead shriek. The deafening noise of aerial bombing penetrates our room. She pulls on the belt of her long white robe.

Manek and Sabcia, my younger brother and sister, dash into the dining room. "Planes attacking! What do you see?" Sabcia asks.

"Dive-bombers coming in low. Swastikas," I answer.

"They'll kill us," Sabcia cries out.

"No!" Milek shouts above the roar. "Planes are heading towards the airport."

Planes overhead shriek. The glass window shakes so hard I think it will shatter to pieces. Quickly, we move away.

"Let's look out of the living room window," Sabcia says and takes Mamusia's hand.

We hurry past the small apartment hallway. Sabcia reaches the window, yanks on the shade and strangles the cord.

"Stop. I'll handle it," Milek orders.

My body feels as contorted as the string on the shade. I want answers. How will Poland respond? How will Germany's invasion impact upon us as Jews?

"Jozek, come here." Milek motions to the left side of the shade. We lift it off of the hooks and lay the shade down in front of the green armchair. Milek pushes the window up and extends his head out. A rush of morning air combined with the boom of engines invades our living room.

"We can get a better view from Mamusia's bedroom," Manek says darting to the doorway.

We crowd in front of Mamusia's window and stare out at the cloudless sky. One window or another makes no difference to me. The horror of the morning attack reflects in all of them. The sight of Mamusia's unmade bed at the side of the large window unnerves me. It's usually done up with fancy colored pillows layered on top of the white chenille bedspread. Labored breathing overtakes my slim body. A cold sweat snakes down my chest.

Explosions burst in the distance, then silence. We watch low fighter and bomber planes fly overhead. Milek decides to go to the dining room to hear news on the radio. Sabcia follows behind him. Her bare feet smack the dark hardwood floor. Her curly chestnut hair bobs atop the collar of her yellow robe as she tries to keep up with his strides.

"More bomber planes in formation," Manek points out to Mamusia and me. His pale face exposes a mask of fear. The ruddy color is gone. Manek nervously runs his hand through his rumpled dark blond hair.

I stand rooted at the window, looking out, feeling terrified and helpless. My mind is racing. *What can we do?* I have no answer.

I join Sabcia and Milek in the dining room and have a premonition I will never view this room the same.

The cherry wooden oval table and six chairs are in the center of the room. I doubt family meals at the table will be as carefree again. The two twin beds are lined up against the wall where Milek and I sleep. Will I ever be able to sleep peacefully again without the roar of the plane engines?

Against the wall, opposite our beds, are a matching credenza and a small dark wooden table. On the polished table is the crystal radio with a wire antenna Milek built. The homemade wireless picks up shortwave transmissions. The pale green wallpaper conceals the electric wiring.

The radio is our connection to the outside. It's now the most important thing in the room. I grab a pair of earphones off of the hook on the wall. My sister and brother listen from the other pair. The announcer's voice blares, "The Luftwaffe are attacking… airport under attack…receiving reports…terminal's roof ripping."

"Attacking the airport. We're safe here," I say with a confidence I do not possess.

"Quiet, Jozek," Milek orders me. He turns the radio's knob to increase the volume.

"There's static. I can't hear." I pound the radio trying to get clearer reception.

"Stop!" Milek yells and shoves my hand away. "You'll break it."

"Milek, calm down."

"Don't tell me what to do, Jozek."

"Okay. Okay." I walk away from the radio to the window and shield my eyes from the sun-dazzled morning. My skin is clammy. My hair and neck are drenched with droplets of sweat. What will become of our lives?

Yesterday after work in the fur shop, I took a twenty-minute train ride to Wielezka, a small town outside of Krakow. I teach pattern making to my boss' friend. It's an easy way to earn extra money, money my family can use.

The clicking of the train's wheels on my trip back was disturbed by a commotion in front of the car. The conductor was shouting and waving his hands. His remarks were repeated up the aisle, "Germans are crossing the border, crossing into Krakow."

The *Kurier Narodowy* newspaper reported the Germans were amassing armored troops along the side of our border. Germany demanded our government allow them a corridor inside the predominately German Polish city of Gdansk. Our government refused. Gdansk gives Poland access to the sea.

Clearly Poland needs outside help. We can't fight alone. Our army is no match for the German army. My family, friends, and I thought a Nazi takeover was slight because Poland has a treaty with France and England. We felt these two countries would be forced to come to our rescue. How could we be so stupid thinking the treaty would stop Germany from attacking?

Never before in my twenty years have I been so scared. Not even last year when I agonized about how we would survive after our Tatus' death. Stroke was listed on the death certificate. But I know all the Jew hating heaped upon him was the cause of his death. The Polish people ratcheted up their hate from curses to hurling sticks and stones. They made it impossible for Tatus to keep his business going.

He was our sole provider and did well financially. We lived a good life. On Sundays, Tatus hired transportation that took us out of town for day trips. We had money for specialty foods and nice clothing.

All that has ended. Since his death, we have to live on Milek's, Sabcia's, and my paychecks. We give our salaries to Mamusia to pay for rent and food and to keep our family intact.

Milek, twenty-two, is employed as an engineer in a metal shop owned by our father's best friend. He previously attended a two-year vocational technical school.

Sabcia, almost eighteen, had to quit high school because there was no money after Tatus died. She enrolled in a Jewish vocational school where she learned dressmaking. She works as a seamstress in a high-end clothing store making wedding and custom gowns for formal occasions.

I contribute with earnings from my furrier job in my mother's cousin's shop. I finished high school last year and went to a technical school to study the furrier trade.

Manek, fourteen, attends high school and is becoming proficient as a tailor. It costs money to attend high school in Poland, yet another toll on our depleted finances.

Our third floor apartment is in a four-story apartment house, which consists of two side-by-side buildings. The buildings on the street form a continuous line with small shops on the corners. We live in Kazimierz, a large Jewish community. At one end a long narrow park separates Kazimierz from the rest of Krakow. Our home is about one block from the park. Krakow is one of the oldest and largest cities in Poland and dates back to the seventh century.

Boom! Boom! I jerk back from the window and trip over my feet. "*Psiakrew*," Goddamn, I curse under my breath.

"What do you hear?" I question Milek and Sabcia still listening to the radio.

"Bombing, almost 33 kilometers west, 20½ miles. Germans are crossing the border, coming toward Krakow," Milek answers.

"*Psiakrew*," I curse out loud this time. I pivot to look out the window. Germany's attack on Krakow raises our vulnerability to the already rampant loathing of Jews in Poland. I hear about pogroms against Jews in Poland's small towns and villages. There is talk about boys in school spat upon and taunted with "T*y parszywy Zyd*", Dirty Jew. We don't experience this in our town. We get along well with non-Jews in our neighborhood.

Yes, there are Jews beaten in Krakow. But we don't have mass destruction of Jewish life and property like that which occurred in Germany and Austria on *Kristallnacht,* the Night of Broken Glass, on November 9, 1938.

What we do have is a ban prohibiting Jews from participating in most trades. Imposed quotas make it difficult for us to get a college education. Somehow we live with this.

"If war erupts, it will mean the extermination of European Jews," Hitler said in his Reichstag speech. As frightening as his words were, it didn't give us the impetus to leave our homes. Today's attack is different. We are under fire with bombs, not words. Why have we Jews been so stubbornly naïve in not recognizing Hitler's evil? We didn't pay enough attention. We wanted to believe Poland was safe from his ranting.

"Planes are coming in low. What do you hear on the radio?" Manek asks as he and Mamusia hurry into the room.

"I'll repeat what I told Jozek," Milek says. "It's not good. There's bombing, almost 33 kilometers west. Germans are crossing the border and moving toward Krakow."

Tears from Sabcia's amber-colored eyes drip to her cheeks. She wipes them away with the initialed handkerchief Mamusia embroidered for her.

"We'll be all right," I say wanting to comfort my sister.

"No. No, Jozek. Not with bombers coming into Krakow," Mamusia fearfully shakes her head.

"We're Jews, but we're Polish too," I point out. I don't really believe what I am saying. I know being Polish won't help us.

"Your father was a patriotic man. He fought in the Austrian Cavalry, the war to end all wars. What did he get for his loyalty? A horse threw him. He came home from the war with a limp that affected him all his life. It's not good for the Jews."

It's not like Mamusia to be bitter. She's the glue that holds us together. When we first heard news about increased assaults against Jews in Germany, she cautioned us not to overact.

Soon after, "Don't buy from the Jews" became the order of the day and was openly preached in churches. Tatus owned a store in the downtown business section near Krakow's small city square. He sold gifts, such as fruit baskets, imported chocolates, and canned fish. When I close my eyes, I can sniff the rich aroma of fresh chocolates and see shoppers' smiles as they choose their selections.

Tatus' workday began at seven in the morning and ended about ten at night. One employee helped him. A wall divided the one-room store to create a separate place for inventory and storage. Mamusia worked in the store when Tatus traveled. She enjoyed the exchange with customers by stepping out from behind the counter and conversing in Polish. She knew their names and asked about their families. They sensed she cared. They in turn treated us as good neighbors. We had no reason to doubt their virtue.

During harvest season, late summer and early fall, Tatus bought fruit from farmers. He traveled to their orchards, in various villages outside the city, by horse and buggy with two hired men. Tatus and his employees would strip the trees and load the fruit onto the wagon. He sold the fruit to owners of chocolate, candy, and marmalade factories.

When Tatus came home from work one day, he told us a Polish orchard owner had beaten him on his back with a stick. The orchard owner called him *"Ty parszywy Zyd"* and told him never to come back again.

"It's no longer safe," Milek warned.

"He's only one owner," Tatus said.

But the tide kept turning. In weeks ahead, one owner became two, two became three, three became four.

Tatus lost contracts to sell farm products to factory owners he had done business with for more than twenty years.

I overheard him telling Mamusia, "I've always been fair. I had good customers. Now they're gone. There's no business from the factories and less and less in the store."

The hatred started when Tatus was alive. I expect the intense dislike of Jews to get worse.

Mamusia did her best to reassure Tatus. She argued his business would turn around. It didn't. Tatus poured all of his savings into the store. In late 1936, at fifty-three-years of age, he was forced to close down the business he worked so hard to create. We were heartbroken to watch him.

Crushed, Tatus tried shielding his anguish by covering his face as he sat in his chair. Only the bald spot in front of his head, framed by his streaked graying brown hair, was visible.

Words couldn't console him. He was a proud man. His good looks and lean body aged before our eyes. Without his life's work and unable to find another means of earning income, he lost interest in living. Two years later Tatus died a broken man.

"Damn. Radio's gone dead!" Milek shouts.

All contact with the outside world is severed. What do we do now?

Chapter 2

A Terrifying Dream with a Horrible Ending

Hanka

The roar of fighter and bomber planes over our apartment building sounds like a terrifying dream with a horrible ending. I hide in the crowded dank cellar with my family. My short dark brown hair is damp with perspiration. Sweat collects on my palms, under my arms, and trickles down my cheeks. The air is saturated with mixed smells of apartment dwellers' bodies and moisture-laden air of the surrounding area.

"Hanka, we'll be all right." A weak smile creases Tatus' face as our matched walnut-colored eyes connect. His fingers nervously massage his trimmed mustache. The air wets Tatus' slick brown hair parted to the side.

Families huddle together. Children's cries are faint sounds lost in the blasts of sirens, fighter planes, and explosions. Then silence.

Mamusia's brown eyes fix her attention on me. "Hanka, come help."

Her brunette hair glimmers in the cellar's darkness. She has it pulled tight in a bun at the back of her head, how I like it. The blue dress pulls snug against her body.

I place my unopened book, *Gone With the Wind*, on the blanket on a damp cellar floor. I pick up plates and help Mamusia dish out roast chicken and duck to our family. The food is in a covered basket on a wooden bench. Mamusia keeps a kosher home. We store slaughtered chickens and geese for food on a terrace off of our apartment kitchen.

Manek, my seventeen-year-old brother, and Tatus carried the basket and bench from the terrace down the steps to the cellar when sirens sounded a steady whirl of all clear.

Before the rush of more fighter planes, we hurried back to our apartment. I took my book. Manek grabbed a deck of cards. Roman picked up his metal Fiat car. My little brother, Roman, is six. I'm fourteen.

I bite off a piece of roast chicken and glance down at my clothes. I'm wearing a white sailor blouse and a navy-blue pleated skirt. It's my school uniform. How did that take place? In haste, I had snatched the first clothes I saw hanging in my closet.

School was supposed to start this Monday. I tuck a strand of hair behind my ears and hold back tears. Last year my favorite subject was history, the semester before it was literature. We see the girls' high school building across the street from our living room balcony.

It started at dawn. The screech of sirens woke me from sleep in my daybed sofa in the large living room. My foot caught in the floral green blanket when I scrambled out of bed and steadied myself from falling. Half asleep, I took out underwear from the dresser drawer and pulled clothes off of hangers. My brothers ran into the living room from their shared bedroom. They wore shorts and partially unbuttoned short sleeve shirts.

"They're attacking. They're attacking," I repeated. I bent down to put on short white socks and slip on white leather loafers. Tatus yelled from the hallway door for us to hurry.

Fear mixed with hope had my head pounding. "Will we be okay?" I called out to Tatus.

"Yes. Come, come." He waved us on to the entrance of our three-room apartment.

"No time for talk. Hurry," Mamusia said directing us to the steps.

We took flight with others from our second floor in an apartment building located in Kazimierz, Krakow's Jewish section. My friend, Helena, and her family were ahead of us clinging to the railings. People ran out of their apartments and rapidly made their way to the cellar. We were all part of an exodus pounding the stairs to the cellar for safety.

We sit on blankets on the cold cement floor, where the floor is cleaner, away from the cubicle for coal storage. The musty smell of ashes absorbed in the walls wraps its odor around us.

"Eat, you will feel better," Tatus says. His warm heart outshines his five-feet-eight-inches body.

"How can I eat? We're being attacked."

"It will end soon."

"Then what? What happens to us after the invasion? The Poles hate us too. Remember when we came out of shul on Shabbos, they mocked us. They stood along the sidewalk shouting, '*Patrzeć, Zydzi*!' Look, Jews! The Polish people look down on us. I see the disgust in their eyes."

"It's not new. We have lived through anti-Semitism before."

Tatus is attempting to allay our fears, but it's not easy dismissing the hatred directed towards Jews.

"I wanted to kick their faces in," Manek says. His brown eyes drip from perspiration as he wipes his gold-wire round eyeglasses with his handkerchief.

"I wish you had," I comment.

"Tatus, you're right," my brother says. "You told us to walk away."

Manek never wants to get Tatus upset. I nibble on another piece of chicken and think back on happier times. I remember helping Mamusia and Bronka, our Polish Catholic live-in housekeeper, prepare for our Shabbos meals. Bronka also took care of Roman. She left our home to go back to her parents' house when Germany was poised to cross the Polish border. We still regard her as a member of our family.

Most of our family lives in Krakow. After synagogue services, we gather together at our grandparents, Aryeh and Sara Ferber's, home. They have eight sons and a daughter, including my father. Manek always wants to end Shabbos early on a Saturday evening to go out on a date. Our parents are religious and forbid him to leave before sundown. He knows this but keeps on asking. He hopes one day he'll get lucky.

My parents entertain family and friends in our apartment after Shabbos ends. I help put out desserts. My favorites are *paczek*, a round spongy yeast cake stuffed with strawberry or chocolate filling and *chrust*, a sweet crisp cake in the shape of a bow.

They play a game called Sixty-Six. Usually there are enough players to sit at five tables. Serious players concentrate on the cards and like to do without all the conversation. These players become tense and impatient when the game slows down. The game's goal is to score sixty-six points by winning tricks where certain cards beat other cards and by announcing marriages of cards, like kings to queens.

Bronka would take Roman with her to the big cathedral church on Sundays. She made the sign of the cross, and Roman sat next to her in the pew. He went to church with her so many times he recited all of the Latin prayers. Bronka beamed at him when she told us this. I smile when I think of Roman in church following along with the service. He's a good student. He attends a religious school and knows how to read and write Polish and Yiddish.

After services, Bronka and Roman would go to the park. He played soccer with the children. She would keep watch from her perch on a bench. Manek and I were also at the park, but we socialized with our own friends.

Will my family ever get back these happy times? Will I be wearing my school clothes again to attend school? Suddenly, I'm jolted out of my reverie.

Sirens blast! My ears ring. Children cry. Bomber planes buzz overhead. Tatus holds onto Roman's hand. He, the mischievous spoiled kid of the family, does not cry while tears cast a wet veil over my eyes.

My pulse quickens. From radios scattered across the cellar, we hear reports of fighting in the cloudless sky. Where are the bombs striking?

"Explosions sound closer!" Mamusia exclaims.

Someone nearby shouts to Tatus, "Leon, it must have struck the trolley line!"

The trolley line is three blocks from our apartment.

"Could be the electrical generating station," Tatus calls back.

Oh, no. The station is next to our apartment building on Waska Street. Will they bomb this building?

Answers to what happens next hang in the humid air. Newsreels at the movies show Adolph Hitler speaking at huge rallies. He blames Jews for all of his country's problems. Hitler's shrill voice on the screen sends shivers up and down my spine.

My parents rationalize Jews have dealt with tyrants before. They say things will end up okay for the Jews. I don't know if I agree with them. I want to believe they're right. Hitler scares me. He sickens me. He's evil.

We wait with others for the all-clear siren to signal it's safe to go back to our apartments. I want to escape the harrowing noise. I wish I could pull my blanket over my head and lie in bed and not sit on a damp hard cement floor. I need things to be as they were before the bombing. I can't fool myself. They won't.

From a shortwave radio, an alert: "German forces, heavy fighting. Polish army is fighting. German forces are attacking."

We are at war.

Chapter 3

A Time for Action

Jozek

It's crucial for us to get out of Krakow. After much deliberation, our best plan is to cross the Hungarian border and be under Russian control. Mamusia agrees my brothers and I should leave but says she and Sabcia will stay. She rationalizes that historically women have not been considered enemies of the State and put into prisons. She insists the war will end in a few weeks.

"Why take the chance women will be safe? We don't know what the Germans will do," I say.

"We'll listen to what the rabbi tells us tomorrow. Then we will make plans."

Who's Mamusia kidding? Her mind is made up.

Saturday morning we dress in our Shabbos clothing. It's hard to break habits even in the worst of times. I wear my white shirt and put on my light wool custom powder-blue suit, my favorite color. A pair of black shoes, not my everyday brown ones, completes the outfit and adds to my five-feet-eight-inches height.

I check that my blue and white tie is straight as I inspect myself in the bathroom mirror. Dark brown hair complements my summer tan. Serious light brown eyes catch me wetting thin lips on my shaved face. Is that a look of apprehension? Mustn't let Mamusia see me scared.

When Tatus was alive, every spring before Passover and every fall before Rosh Hashanah, we were all outfitted with new clothing. This suit will have to last. Don't know when we'll be able to afford new clothes again.

On the way to the synagogue, I finger leftover peanuts in my pants pocket. Mamusia fusses over me. She stuffs nuts into my pocket when I leave home. She complains I'm too skinny.

Several hundred members of the orthodox *Old Synagoga*, Old Synagogue, fill the sanctuary. A buzz of noise cascades around the main prayer room.

"Quiet. Please. Quiet," our seventy-plus-year-old rabbi orders during the service. "Show respect for the Torah."

Three Torahs are uncovered and carried by synagogue leaders in a line down one wooden aisle and up another. Worshippers stand close to the aisles and touch their *talleisim*, Jewish prayer shawls, to the Torahs and to their lips. The leaders walk five white stone steps up on two side stairs to the *bima*, the platform from which the Torah is read.

A black wrought iron gazebo in the center of the room surrounds the *bimah*. A black iron chandelier, framed with candlesticks, casts light on one of the Torahs placed on a table on the *bimah*. The reader, wearing a prayer shawl, bows his head and begins chanting the Torah portion.

My mind wanders. I hear Tatus reading from the Torah on the bimah, his voice strong and melodic. Finished, he lifts his head up and seeks out Mamusia in the women's prayer room in the balcony. She parts the lace curtain above the railing and acknowledges him with a slight sway of her head. Her black hat exposes her round face and strands of pulled-back brown hair. Her arched eyebrows enhance her brown eyes dotted with a touch of green.

We pray here on Shabbos and Jewish holidays. Praying in the synagogue is not the same without Tatus. I miss him. During the week when Tatus was alive, we prayed closer to our home at *Remuh Synagoga*, a small synagogue that has an adjacent cemetery.

Should I leave Kazimierz? I ask myself. Yes, I answer, terrified of what the Germans will do to us. No, I answer, guilty about leaving my mother and sister behind.

Decide. Guilt is not easy to dismiss. My throat closes up. My chest tightens. I shield my face with my hands and talk silently to Papa. What do you say? Help me.

Listen to Milek, I imagine he counsels. Milek, the oldest at twenty-two, is two years older than I am. Sabcia is almost eighteen. Manek, the youngest, is fourteen. Since Tatus died, Milek is the head of our family.

We stand as the Torah is raised, covered, and returned to the Ark, where the Torah scrolls are kept. Rows of men wearing prayer shawls on their shoulders and yarmulkes, skullcaps, on their heads recite ancient Hebrew prayers. Voices from women and children float down from the balcony. I'm a good student of the Torah and join in by rote and with my heart.

When my brothers and I were younger, a teacher came to our apartment during the week to teach us Hebrew lessons. Tatus patted my head after I recited the prayers. He was proud of my religious studies.

Milek's slim body fidgets on the wooden bench. Morning sun pours in through the windows and highlights his freckled face. We sit with friends in a row in the middle section, near the rear of the synagogue. Our friends are of one mind to escape from Krakow. I whisper to Milek my anguish of leaving Mamusia and Sabcia behind. Go? Stay? The questions burn at the pit of my stomach.

Our rabbi stands erect on the bima. He's a strong orator, and I'm anxious to hear what he'll say. I hope his words will make an impact on Mamusia to leave. Will he have something new to impart?

He clears his throat and casts his eyes over the packed sanctuary. The rabbi towers over the red velvet pulpit and adjusts his black hat. Gray payos, side curls, hang down sides of his face. He tugs at his trimmed gray beard and asks the ushers to close the hallway doors. A hush settles over the room.

"My friends," he begins leaning forward and gripping the pulpit, "we must not panic in the face of this invasion. We Jews are Polish people. The government will protect us. G-d will protect us."

Where was G-d when Tatus was called a dirty Jew and beaten? I am silent. One doesn't show disrespect to the rabbi.

"Jewish people lived through pogroms before. We shall do so again." His voice climbs to a higher pitch.

"We must not lose faith." He waves his right fist in the air. "We will survive this invasion."

How will we do it? I sourly think. This is not a pogrom. This is war.

"Faith alone won't save us," a man mutters, sitting in the row directly in back of me.

He's right. We need a lot more than faith. We need help from the British and the French. They need to honor their treaty with Poland.

His sermon ended, the rabbi asks for silence and proceeds with the service. "Rise for the Mourner's Kaddish, prayer said in honor of the deceased. *Yit'gadal v'yit'kadash Sh'mei raba…*"

"How can we go without Mamusia and Sabcia?" I question Milek at the service's conclusion. "We would be abandoning them."

Before Milek can reply, Manek joins us from across the aisle. "It's not safe to stay. My friends plan to escape while they can," he reports.

"Jozek, listen to reason," Milek says.

"Maybe Mamusia will leave if we insist we need to be together," I wistfully answer. "Then Sabcia will come too."

"Forget it. Insisting Mamusia should come won't budge her. I doubt if anything we say will convince her to change her mind. You heard the sermon, our rabbi hasn't given her a reason to flee from Poland," Milek says.

We walk down the hallway to meet Mamusia and Sabcia at the bottom of the balcony steps. In uneven lines, we join with congregants and step down creaky wooden stairs to a large auditorium for the blessing over wine for the Kiddush. Our cantor chants the blessing,"*Baruch atah…*"

The customary drinking of wine and grape juice and the eating of slices of cakes and cookies does not evolve into the usual joy and conviviality. With nothing more to be learned, we're anxious to go home.

"Rosalia, what will you do?" Mamusia's friend asks her before we head for the steps.

"Do, do nothing. The boys will go. Sabcia and I will stay."

She's stubborn.

Her friend shakes her head. "I don't want to go either, but I'm not sure. Maybe we won't be safe here."

"You have to decide for yourself. I feel women and girls will not be harmed."

Her friend is open to leaving. Why can't Mamusia be like her?

We follow with others up the wooden stairs to the synagogue exit. Usually we'd visit with relatives after services. Shabbos is a day of rest and enjoyment but not today. Today is a time to plan, a time for action.

Milek gives it a try and appeals to Mamusia to leave as we walk toward our apartment building. He voices his concern that we need to be together.

She senses my indecision and squeezes my left arm. "Jozek,

go. When things quiet down, it will be safe to return. I'll only slow you down. Sabcia will be with me." My sister nods her head in agreement, but her frightened eyes show her true feelings.

"Jozek," Milek says, "we must get to the Hungarian border before it's impossible to get out of Krakow. This is a significant fact we can't ignore."

He's losing his patience with me. Milek forcefully pushes the button more than once to the lift in our building and opens the shiny brass door to the cage when it arrives.

"I'll go," I say stepping into the lift.

Stating I will flee with my brothers doesn't free me from guilt. We're a close family. The fear of the unknown, of what will happen to Jewish boys and men left in Krakow, terrifies me.

Tatus would never have allowed our family to remain separated and neither will I. As I grab the handle and pull aside the lift's door to step out onto our apartment floor, I make a silent promise to myself. I will be back for Mamusia and Sabcia before long.

Chapter 4

Day Three – We Have a Place to Stay

Jozek

Sunday, September third, my brothers and I leave at the crack of dawn and join the mass exodus composed of almost all Jewish males. Our plan is to head east toward the Hungarian border occupied by the Russian forces, close to 250 kilometers, about 155 miles.

It's unusually hot. We wear cotton pants and short sleeve shirts and carry few belongings in our knapsacks. We expect to be back before cold weather sets in.

We walk amid thousands of people, wagons, and horses on jammed paved roads. We are shoved forward with others in no particular order. We walk from farm to town, town to farm, mostly at night, to hide from German planes and their machine guns. By day we sleep hidden in fields, under trees, and in potato patches.

For food, we eat what we pick from the farms, such as potatoes, carrots, and beets. Sometimes we are lucky and manage to find tomatoes. I miss eating the nuts Mamusia puts inside my pants pockets.

"Damn. It's all mud," Milek says turning the bucket attached to a rope and chain upside down.

"Give it to me." I take the bucket from Milek and look down. It's dry from the volume of people drinking water.

"We'll come across another well," I say trying to be positive, but not knowing if we will. Thirsty, throats burning, and hot clothing pressing against our perspiring bodies, my brothers and I trudge on.

Along the way, we learn France and Great Britain have declared war on Germany. Our spirits are lifted by the news. The French army is the strongest in Europe. The British rule the seas. With their help, the war should end quickly. Soon we will be able to return home to Mamusia and Sabcia.

After walking about 56 kilometers, roughly 35 miles, from Krakow, we decide to stop at the home of Tatus' friends. The married couple and their two sons live in a house on the outskirts of Bochnia, a small town known for its salt mines. We never met them but hope they'll take us in for the night.

Darkness surrounds us like a cloak when Manek knocks on the front door of their single home. One of the couple's sons opens the door, and we introduce ourselves. He tells his parents, who are standing with their younger son in the shadow of the hallway light, to let us come inside.

A whiff of the aroma of cooked chicken reminds me of home. The wife must sense our hunger because she quickly escorts us into her kitchen and asks us to sit down at the white wooden table and chairs. White wooden cabinets line two of the walls of this well-lit appealing room. Helped by her sons, she puts out some leftover chicken, thick potato soup, bread and butter, and tea on the table.

My brothers and I hesitate to partake of the food in front of us. We are thankful for the food, but it's not kosher. We look at each other. Milek is the first to pile the food on his plate. Manek and I follow. We avoid adding butter to the bread. It's something we don't do. According to Jewish dietary laws, meat and dairy are not to be eaten together. I rationalize to myself that G-d will forgive us for eating the non-kosher food. We don't know when we will have our next meal. We need to keep up our strength.

The meal stifles growls in our stomachs and aches in our throats. Eating home cooked food and the sensation of seeing their family together floods my mind with what we have lost. We are fleeing not only from the Germans but also from our everyday life.

We answer questions from the husband about Germany's invasion of Krakow. Soon after we finish eating, the sons hand us blankets to sleep on the wooden floor in the hallway behind the entrance. Their house gives me a pretense of safety. I instantly fall asleep.

"Get up! Get up, the Germans are coming!" A kerosene lamp shines in our eyes as the husband conveys the urgent news.

"What? Where?" Milek asks as we shield our eyes from the lamp.

"News on the radio. Germans are coming from the south. Quick, you must leave."

We step into our shoes. It's four a.m. His wife enters the hallway and hands bread and apples for us to Manek. The sons, awakened by their father's commotion, stare down at us from the top of the stairs.

We barely have time to thank the family for their hospitality before rushing out the door. I gave no thought as to whether they were Christians or not when we stopped at their house. Now that I know, it was courageous of them to let us stay. I'm happy Tatus was so well respected by some of his non-Jewish friends.

We stop not far from the house. "Now what?" I ask, fully awake.

"Change of strategy," Milek says. "We'll shift our plan from walking on main roads to going through villages and fields. This way we'll avoid the mass of people."

Germany occupies Czechoslovakia south of Poland. Germans are advancing not only from the west but also from the south. Milek's idea is to go north, then head northeast to the Hungarian border, because the roads we have been on lead to muddy water and less food.

With Milek's compass as our guide, we detour north until we reach the highway. We find more available food and less people walking. Water in the wells is not used up as quickly. Friendly farmers give us hot soup to eat and water to wash with. There are still decent Polish people left. Not all of them hate Jews. This course is also less dangerous than before because Germans are bombing roads and bridges, not villages. At least, from this perspective, we feel less exposed to the enemy.

Sweat drips hot beads onto our bodies and faces. After going north, we go east until we encounter the Red Army soldiers. My body relaxes when we reach the area. We made it. In the two weeks since we started our journey from Krakow, we have walked about 200 kilometers, over 124 miles. Once we are out of German control, into the Russian-Occupied part of Poland, we believe we will have succeeded in escaping from immediate danger.

We come to a standstill with other men at the Hungarian border. "Look ahead." Milek shields his eyes from the sun and points at Russian guards with their rifles. "The border is closed."

"No, can't be," I say. I walk ahead towards a man closer to the border and tap him on his shoulder. "Why is no one moving?"

"Russian soldiers forbid anyone else to cross. If you had reached the border a day earlier, you would have made it into Hungary."

"No one can get across?"

"No one. We are too late."

"Damn."

No need to tell my brothers what is happening. They had come up to us and overheard what the man said. My brothers' troubled faces tell it all. Exhausted, I move back and find some empty space. I plop to the ground. I remove my dusty shoes and massage blistered sore feet. Baked by the sun, Milek and Manek join me on grass matted by the footsteps of others.

"My back aches," Manek says stretching out on the grass, hands behind his head.

"What about your feet? Mine are burning," I say.

"Mine too. I need to rest."

"Rest, but not for long. We must decide our next move," Milek says.

What to do? Before the invasion, I lived a contented life with my family and had a good job. Most of my free time was spent with friends. We hung out at the sports club, played soccer in a field, and swam in the river. We drank coffee in cafes and sat around for small talk. Now I'm on the run. The sweat of summer and fear of the unknown coat my body like paint.

After a brief rest, Milek stands and shields his eyes from the sunlight. "I have a plan. We will go to Leopoldynow."

"Why Leopoldynow? Will it be safe?" I ask. I dust off my pants streaked with grass.

"What other choices do we have?" he asks me.

Milek is right. What choices do we have? The Hungarian border is closed. It's not safe to go home. Where else can we go to escape from the Germans?

We begin our walk toward Leopoldynow, a Zionist farm in eastern Poland. Our brother is a member of Akiba, the organization managing Leopoldynow. We try to stay positive and lighthearted. Manek and I tease Milek about the beating sun creating more freckles on his face. Usually a sore point with him, today he laughs it off. He thinks girls don't like them.

Milek and I tease our younger brother about playing ping-pong. Manek rarely wins games. I excel at ping-pong and soccer. I am also the strongest swimmer. My brothers joke about me jumping into the water without looking first. Last time I did this, I crashed into a girl in the river. She laughed as we collided. We do our best underneath our banter to disguise our worry about Mamusia and Sabcia.

"Milek, Tatus never liked you belonging to Akiba," I say.

"He worried. He thought I would go to Palestine. I told him I wouldn't, but that the Jews need their own country."

"Did Tatus believe you, about not going?" I ask.

"Sure. Why not?"

"Would you have gone?"

"Not then."

I hate that I didn't stay with Mamusia and Sabcia and admit to my brothers that I was afraid.

"You were right to leave. It isn't safe to stay in Krakow," Milek tries to reassure me.

"I miss them. Nothing better happen to them," Manek says. He forms his fists like a fighter ready to swing a punch.

"Take it easy. Don't get carried away. You're not ready to fight," Milek chuckles.

"I could fight."

"Relax. We don't have to fight."

At last, drained from walking and the danger of being shot at by Germans, we reach Leopoldynow. A guard outside the gate blocks us from entering. He explains the farm is over its limit with an influx of people from the western part of Poland. Its capacity of thirty trainees has swollen to more than one hundred people.

Apologetic, he says he's sorry, but there's no room for anyone else. Before he can turn us away, Milek names two friends who live on the farm. The sentry guard motions to a guard inside the gate and gives him the names of Milek's friends. He asks the guard to bring one of them to the gate. Thanks to Milek's friend and my brother's involvement with Akiba, we're allowed into the farm.

Finally we have a place to stay. I drop my smelly, hot, weary body down on some straw in a corner of a wooden barrack. Before long I'm sound asleep.

Leopoldynow is used to train young people in agricultural skills who will immigrate to Palestine and work on a kibbutz. A wealthy Jewish family donated the land outside a small town called Rava-Ruska. It's a stopover on the Lwow-Warsaw railroad line.

Because the farm cannot support the extra one hundred or so people, we need to bring in income. Leaders divide everyone into four groups. One group works on the farm. The second group sells products grown on the farm. The third group sells their services to other farmers. The fourth group, the organizers, is responsible for going to bigger towns in the area to obtain needed items. I am one of the organizers.

Chapter 5

Day Eight - August to September from Happiness to Despair

Frania

I hold my son's small hand as we walk into the living room. "Henryk, Wilus is ready for his bedtime story."

"What should we read tonight, Wilus?" My husband shuts off the radio and rises from the rocking chair.

"*Krolick*, Rabbit."

"We read that book last night. Not a different one?"

"*Krolick*. It's my best story."

"Then *krolick* it is," Henryk agrees.

He takes the picture book from the top shelf of the walnut wooden bookcase standing against the wall and places our three-year-old son on his lap. I listen to his subdued voice as I withdraw from the room. From all appearances it looks like an ordinary evening, but it's not.

Muffling sobs while catching warm tears on the back of my hand, I walk into our kitchen. I wipe my moist hand with Wilus' napkin left on the kitchen table and discard it into the corner trashcan. While I take the plate and glass from his snack to the sink, my mind revolves elsewhere. *What do the Germans want from the Jews? What will they do to us? What happens now?*

Sirens and the roar of fighter-bomber planes still screech in my head. I dry the dishes and shudder as I remember when we fled to the basement to take cover. I stopped on the stairs and held onto the railing, my knees weakened from fear.

I have to compose myself. I shouldn't be crying. I need to be strong for Wilus. I sit down at the rectangular kitchen table situated against the wall near our balcony door.

Henryk has built up a solid tailor shop business sewing women's clothing, mostly suits. Before the German invasion of Krakow, life was good. Now our world has been turned upside down. From August to September, I've gone from happiness to despair.

I enter the living room and smile at my family. Henryk is asking Wilus what part of the book he likes best.

"Don't know, Tatus."

"What makes the story good?"

"*Krolick* plays soccer."

"Let's see, do your ears flap like *krolick's*?" Henryk pulls on Wilus' earlobes.

"Silly, I'm not a *krolick*."

"Are you sure? Let's see. Do your ears wiggle?"

"You're making them wiggle," Wilus giggles.

Henryk takes Wilus off of his lap and stands up. "Bedtime. I'll call Mamusia," Henryk says before he notices me.

He bends down on his knee and looks into Wilus' face. He orders him to be silent and raises his voice to emphasize to him that he's not to call out to us after he goes into his bedroom. He tells him not to worry. He is safe.

"Finished with the story?" I ask, quietly, on purpose to soften Henryk's command.

"Yes, Mamusia."

"Then time for bed," I say running my hands through his dark brown hair. The three of us walk to the upright tall storage cabinet. The dark wooden furniture conceals Wilus' bedroom door. In one swift movement, Henryk and I push aside the mostly empty cabinet.

Before Wilus and I enter into his room, he looks up at Henryk and asks, "Will the bad soldiers come here, Tatus?"

"No. I told you before. You don't have to be afraid. You are safe."

"Noises outside scare me."

"Ignore the noises. I need you to listen to me, Wilus. It's important for you to be quiet. You understand?"

"Can we go on a train ride again?"

"Yes," Henryk says. *Damn them. I'm forced to tell my son a lie.*

"Time for bed," I say putting an end to their conversation. I lead our son inside his bedroom to his bed. I sit him down on top of his light blue blanket and start to help him change into his pajamas.

"I can do it." He pushes my hands away and pulls on his blue and red pajamas shorts. He struggles but manages to put his hands into the short sleeves of the pajamas' top.

"See. I did it myself."

"Yes, you did. You're a big boy." I reach over and smooth his pajamas' top down. I cover him and position his brown frayed teddy bear next to him on the white covered pillow. I kiss him on the top of his head.

"Can I have my train?" He sits up and asks.

"All right. I'll get it for you."

He's delaying going to sleep. Who can blame him? He shouldn't have to sleep closed in like this. The new wooden toy box Henryk made for him, filled to the brim with toys, is to the right of the doorway. I push aside toys he once couldn't be without and bring him his metal train car.

"Tatus says he will take me on a train ride."

"If he says he will, he will." I tuck him under his cover.

He bounces up. "*Kocham cię*," I love you, Mamusia.

I take him into my arms and hold him tightly against my chest. "I love you, love you. I love you so much."

Once again, I cover him with his blanket. Before I switch off the lamp's light, I glance at the silver-framed photo on his bedside table. We were in the park. Wilus was in his stroller, and I stood beside him. I posed smiling as Henryk took the photo with his camera.

At four months of age, he had thick wavy dark brown hair. I tried patting down his hair, but it kept fluttering in the gentle breeze. Henryk was handsome in his gray suit and hat. Wilus' hazel eyes favor Henryk's while his straight nose and heart-shaped lips are mirror images of mine.

"Choo, choo, choo, choo."

"Shush, do you want me to take your train away? What did Tatus tell you? You must be quiet."

"*Prezepraszam*." Sorry.

"Close your eyes. It's bedtime."

It's dark when Mamusia shuts the door. I don't like to be in the dark by myself. I can't see the hallway light. I want Mamusia to stay. I'm scared of noises from planes in the sky. Mamusia and Tatus say we are safe in our apartment. Sometimes Tatus looks angry with me, and it makes me afraid.

I wish my cousin Roman could come to our apartment to play. Roman gave me a slingshot and showed me how to hit the rats from our balcony. They run around at the bottom of the bakery's wall next door to our building. Bang!

I hit one. Bang! Bang! Roman hits two. He always hits more. I can't play with my slingshot anymore. I'm not allowed on the balcony. I want the bad soldiers to go away.

I wait at the doorway a few minutes until I sense he has fallen asleep. In the hallway, Henryk and I move the cabinet back into place erasing a view of his bedroom door. I straighten the embroidered linen tablecloth and a white cotton blanket on the shelves along with two of Henryk's pants and three sweaters.

"Frania, let's have tea," Henryk says. We walk to the right of Wilus' bedroom and enter the long narrow kitchen off of the foyer.

I'm proud of my husband. His tailor shop trade has increased. At the age of thirty-two, Henryk has become a successful businessman. We rent space for his shop on the ground floor of an apartment building, in a residential area in Kazimierz.

Next to his shop's entryway, he uses a nice-size room as a greeting and waiting area for customers. This room is furnished with three navy-blue velvet-upholstered chairs with two walnut wooden round tables. Matching white glass lamps with white shades trimmed with blue ribbon fringes stand on the tables. A multicolored porcelain bowl on one table and a small glass bowl on the other one, give the room a touch of elegance. Framed photos of beautifully dressed women adorn one of the walls.

Beyond that space is a room where Henryk does consultations. Here is where customers pick out materials from fabric books and styles from photos showing the latest fashions. Henryk also uses this room for fittings. From this room, a door to the right leads to a cutting room.

The largest room, accessible from the cutting room, is the sewing room where two tailors work for him.

At first Henryk worked alone, but now the sewing room has three sewing machines, tables, and mannequins.

It was fun to see Wilus' first reaction to the two mannequins when we came to the shop before opening for business. He wanted to pin one of his wax crayon pictures of a boy in the park onto one of the mannequin's covering. Henryk admonished him before I could tell Wilus the mannequins were for Tatus' work.

Wilus' eyes started to water. I brushed his tears away and made a game of his hiding the picture from me. I took my time circling the room and found his drawing shoved under one of the sewing machine's pedals. I took him in my arms, and we laughed together at his good hiding place.

Women's suits usually need three fittings. Henryk is a perfectionist. I enjoy seeing him nod his head in appreciation when a customer admires his work. Will the Germans permit him to run his business? If not, how will we support ourselves? We are helpless to control our lives.

My hands tingle with fear. I light the stove with a match on the second try. Henryk's arms encircle my waist. He bends his trim five-feet-ten-inches body and kisses my neck below my short hair. I feel the strands from the top of his hair and inhale the faint scent of his masculine sweat.

As if reading my thoughts, he says, "We'll be fine Frania. Relax. Take a deep breath. You're tense. Britain and France declared war on Germany. That's a good thing. The war won't last long."

I cling to Henryk and feel the roughness from his early morning shave. I'm not sure he really believes the war will end soon.

He wipes off tears clouding my eyes with his hand. "Don't cry Frania. We'll be fine. I have hidden gold coins in a suitcase in Wilus' bedroom closet, behind a box of fabric, for emergencies."

The kettle purrs, and I move out of the warmth of his arms to shut off the flame. With practiced motions, I take tea from the top shelf of the wooden pantry at the far end of the kitchen. On the blue and yellow floral tablecloth, I place white porcelain cups and saucers, silverware, and the last of our strawberry-filled pastry. Who knows when I can purchase it again? I bring sugar and napkins from the pale-yellow counter that matches the color of our linoleum floor. What if Britain and France can't stop Hitler? Then what?

"Henryk, I worry about Wilus. He jumps at any noise and complains about the dark. He delays going to sleep because he's so scared."

"I understand, but it's necessary we keep him hidden in his room at night until this is all over."

I watch Henryk stir one heaping spoonful of sugar into his tea while I take a sip of tea from my cup.

"Frania, have you noticed there are times when Wilus stays under the dining room table until I call to him to come out?"

"I thought he stopped doing that."

"No, he hasn't. Do you think he is doing it now because he's scared of the attack? Before, when he hid under the table, I thought it was because he was afraid he did something wrong."

"It's probably a combination of both." I rub my forehead to ease the sunburst appearing in my eyes. A migraine is coming on. I should rest my eyes.

"He's a sensitive child and smart. Noises from the planes scare him. The bombing frightened us. How can we not expect it to affect him? He's just a child. You should have patience and not be so hard with him."

"Damn!" Henryk hits the table with his right hand. "I have to be strict. He needs to obey us. What if those filthy Germans come pounding on our door. Then what? Can't you realize any moving around or sounds from Wilus' room could result in bringing us all harm? We don't know what they will do if they find him. They could take him away. If you don't understand this, how will I get Wilus to listen to me?"

"Henryk, he's only three. You should be calm around him. We need to seem normal. We have to control our fear for his sake."

Henryk reaches across the table and takes my hands in his. "Frania, you do realize there is no normal anymore. Circumstances have changed. There's no going back to before."

"I know that, but I think we should try to keep things the same." My migraine is not going away. I ease my hands away from my husband and massage my forehead.

I look behind him at the ticking black and white clock on the wall below our high ceiling. It shows almost nine o'clock. We are in a waiting period. What will Britain and France do to help the Jews?

Two white shades cover our windows, taped with paper to prevent cracks from explosions. The white lace curtains on top of the shades are drawn closed.

The dimness of the outside cobblestone street is illuminated by the glow from black pole street lamps that sit close to the curbs. Our modern two-bedroom apartment is in the Jewish section. The building is similar to others on the block with yellow stucco fronts, terraces, and ground level stores. We have our pick of an abundance of businesses displaying their hand-painted signs. It's a vibrant area. It's a place where many people shop for pastries, frequent the butcher shop, and linger in cafes.

I miss our open windows. I miss the familiar sweet smells of freshly baked cakes nestling in the air from the bakery on the street.

I take a sip of tea and put my cup down spilling some into the saucer. My hands shake. My mind is full of a panic I cannot erase. I take a deep breath. Eight days ago we had peace. Today we have war. What will the Germans do to us?

Chapter 6

I Become a Kind of Hero

Jozek

By the end of September, Poland is partitioned almost in half between Hitler and Stalin. Russian forces occupy Rava-Ruska. Life is difficult at Leopoldynow. The farmland can't provide enough food for everyone. My brothers and I have no warm clothing to shield us against Poland's colder days and nights.

My committee, the organizers, has the task of exchanging farm goods, such as live chickens, eggs, bread, wheat, and coarse salt to people in Lwow, the nearby larger town. Sales of these goods raise money to buy extra food and supplies.

Germans control the two salt mines outside of Krakow. Suddenly salt has become a hot commodity. One salt mine is east in Wieliczka, almost 7 kilometers, over 4 miles. The other salt mine is east in Bochnia, almost 33 kilometers, 20½ miles, away.

In town one day, I barter chickens with a Hasidic Jew for salt he has hidden away. Committee members help me divide the more than two hundred and twenty pounds of salt and put the salt into knapsacks. We place the knapsacks onto people on bicycles. In exchange for a cup of salt, they get eggs and other products from the farmers. Eventually we obtain enough food to make it worthwhile to take a horse and wagon and go to Lwow to sell the commodities.

Another day after the sale of farm products, three men and I travel to Lwow by train. Our task is to buy gloves, boots, and shovels for the farming committee to harvest potatoes and other products.

The first train car is empty. We take window seats in scattered rows. Trees flash by, colors changing from green to yellow and red. When I stretch my legs out under the seat in front of me, my eyes latch onto the back of the frame and the velvet-material covering. I lean forward to take a closer look at the maroon velvet fabric. I carefully run my hands around the top, bottom, and sides of the velvet covering the metal seat. *It should work*, I think.

Excited and energized, I stand up and look back at the men. "I have a good idea. I can sew gloves out of the velvet on the backs of these seats." Before they can react, I take out a red Swiss Army knife from my pants pocket. "No one is here but us. I can do this."

The three men stand in the aisle while I brace myself and work diligently to the swaying motion of the train. I cut strips of velvet cloth off from the bottom half of the backs of the seats. This way the exposed black metal on the backs of the seats will not be easily visible.

I go from one row of seats to another row of seats and hand velvet strips of material to one man. He hands off the material to the man standing next to him who gives the strips to the next person. The last man puts them into my knapsack on a train seat across the aisle from where I have my train seat.

I am nearly done when, *squeeeeak*, the rear door begins to open. The men rush to take their seats. I cram the strip of velvet in my hands into my knapsack with the other pieces and shove my knife into my pants pocket.

The heavy door swings back behind two Russian policemen patrolling the train. With rifles slung over their shoulders, they walk up the aisle passing the rows where the three men took their seats.

Black shiny leather-booted feet stop at my row. The policeman points to my knapsack, "What do you have here?"

Damn. I left the knapsack on the floor next to my leg. In my haste, I didn't kick the black knapsack under my seat. My eyes dart up to the solidly built tall policeman.

"Nothing much, pieces of material." I mumble.

"Give it here. Why are you on the train?"

"I'm going to town to sell the material," I say nonchalantly while my throat begins to constrict. I hand him the knapsack, and he places it on the seat in the row across from me.

"What's this?" He frowns at me and pulls out strip after strip of the maroon velvet material and holds them up for inspection to the other policeman.

"These are pieces of velvet I will sell in town," I answer politely.

The strips of velvet puzzle the policemen. I have a problem because they don't like my answers. The Russian policeman asks me what is this piece and what is that piece of velvet. I repeat I am going to Lwow to sell the material. He is irritated with my answer. My pulse quickens. Sweat dampens my hands. I'm scared that the longer he questions me he will discover I cut the strips of velvet off from the backs of the metal seats.

"Enough of this, you are going to the police station." Perplexed, he motions for me to proceed down the aisle.

I avert eye contact with my companions from the farm. The policeman escorts me off of the train at the next stop. Carrying my knapsack on his shoulder with his rifle, he gestures for me to step down onto the train platform. The second policeman follows us out.

Fear soars through my body like a plane flying skyward. What have I gotten myself into? The officer pushes me into the back seat of a nearby parked black police car and gets in after me. The other Russian policeman drives the car. In about fifteen minutes, we reach the central police station.

We enter through a main entrance at the front of the building and pass along a hallway with dull brown nicked wooden floors. The policeman ushers me into a large room and places the knapsack onto an empty desk lined up against the wall. I tell myself to keep it simple. It's clear to me he's on a mission to charge me with something. Thank G-d he didn't recognize the velvet material or see where I cut the pieces off of the metal seats.

Bang! A double French door, to the right of the room, opens creating a sharp noise against the walls. A stocky five-feet-tall policeman enters. By the way he carries himself, I sense he is a very important person. He wears a big red band that has a sickle emblem across his chest. I notice his black shiny boots are too big for his feet.

"Jozek, what are you doing here?" He offers me a wide smile and walks towards me, hands on his hips. *How does he know me? Can he help get me out of trouble?*

I look down at him and answer with my ready-made answer. "I was on my way to Lwow," I motion to the policemen, "they took me off of the train. I did nothing wrong. Nothing," I emphasize.

"Why bring him here?" He points his finger at the senior policeman.

"He has these pieces of velvet material."

"Velvet, that's it?"

"He says he's going to sell the velvet material."

"Velvet? What do I care about velvet material? There's no crime here," he snaps at the policeman. "Let him go."

"Yes, of course, Commandant."

The policeman answers him politely, but his venomous eyes show his contempt towards me.

"Jozek, you're free to go." The commandant gives his order and takes leave.

"Thank you," I say to his back. I pick up my knapsack from the table and rush to the exit. No need to give the policemen any time to start trouble with me.

Outside I take a few seconds to gulp in fresh air to clear the acid that fills my throat. As I hurry away from the police station to take the train back to the farm, I ponder how the commandant knows me. Luck is with me. It could have turned ugly.

At Leopoldynow, I design a pattern, then cut and sew strips of the maroon velvet material into gloves.

The story of the gloves, made from strips of material cut from the bottom backs of the train seats, spreads throughout the farm. I become a kind of hero.

Things would have turned out differently if the commandant didn't recognize me. Could he know me from the sports club, my work in the fur shop, or from somewhere else? In any case, he saved me from jail, or something worse. Sometimes good fortune doesn't leave you.

Chapter 7

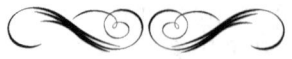

Two Months of Occupation - You Are in Deep Trouble

Jozek

It's November. Life goes on at Leopoldynow. Russians control the area for now. The war has no ending in sight. The Akiba management is in urgent need of money to buy food, clothing, and farm supplies to feed us and combat the harsh cold Polish winter.

I'm never warm. I sleep with hands under my stomach trying to generate some body heat. My brothers and I have holes in the soles of our shoes. Our lightweight clothing is not fit for winter.

Life as I once knew it has changed. It's not entirely my own. I need to do whatever it takes to help keep the farm running. At least we have a place to stay.

Early one Friday morning, another man and I load live chickens and turkeys into a crate and put it onto a horse-pulled wagon. Smells from the fowl cover the crisp smell of the cold air.

We head to the Jewish section of the nearby city to sell the livestock. Our first stop is on the road below a corner two-story house. The man stays with the wagon. I wrap my hand around a turkey's gargling throat and climb the small hill to the pathway. A pleasant middle-aged woman, wearing a flowered apron over her dress, answers the doorbell ring on the white wooden door. She agrees to buy the turkey but wants me to kill it first. She directs me to the back kitchen door. The room has a circular stairway leading to the second floor.

With dim light from a fixture and a window, I step hard on the turkey's head. I make a quick cut at its neck with a sharp knife the woman hands me. Blood splatters. Cursing under my breath, I hand her the dead turkey and ask for rags to wipe the blood off of the green linoleum floor, my clothes, and the knife. I can't present myself to other customers looking like this.

The man from the farm and I move from house-to-house with similar results. Most of the chickens and turkeys are sold when we head back to the farm before Shabbos.

Money continues to be a problem for running the farm. A man in a nearby village has Polish sausages in his home. I negotiate a price with him for one hundred pounds and transport the sausages by horse and wagon to the farm. I divide the sausages up into several buckets with help from my committee members. Four men and I ride in a horse-led wagon to the big town. I drop them off on separate street corners to sell the sausages.

"Sausages, fresh sausages for sale!" I hold the food up high in my hands and wave them to people who pass by the busy street corner. About half of my stock is gone when a heavyset policeman, wearing the hammer and sickle banner over his freshly pressed uniform, rushes up to me. He yanks the sausages out of my hands and throws them into the bucket with the unsold sausages.

"What are you doing here? You can't sell products on street corners. You're forbidden to sell items not available in the stores. You're under arrest."

"Please. Listen. I didn't know I couldn't do this. I had no idea I was doing something unlawful."

He motions with his right hand to a policeman sitting in a car. He tells him to drive us to the police station. Russian Communists control the area. Damn. I will be charged as a black marketeer. The Russian policeman and I get into the back seat of the car with the bucket of unsold sausages between us on the floor. There's little time to dwell upon my precarious situation because the police station is around the corner.

The policeman carries the bucket and ushers me into the building. The driver of the car follows behind me. The police station has one large room. I can see smaller rooms to the far left. I cough at the strong odor of smoked cigarettes. The smell triggers my desire for a cigarette. The arresting officer drops the bucket on an unmanned wooden desk near the front door of the building. He orders me to stop at a nearby table and commands me to empty my pockets. I take out the money from sales of the sausages. I place my red Swiss Army knife and pieces of string onto the table etched with coffee cup rings and cigarette burns. Then I'm told I should turn my pockets inside out.

I do as he says. The other officer picks up the money, my Swiss Army knife, and the string. The arresting officer shoves me by my right shoulder and points me into one of the smaller rooms. Inside the windowless room are a table and three chairs. A bright light fixture hangs over the dark brown unsteady wooden table.

"Sit down. You're in deep trouble," he says.

I need to somehow change his antagonistic view of my situation. I want to appear calm, although my mind conjures a vision of me in a jail cell. The officer pulls out one of the mismatched wooden chairs and sits directly across from me. I straighten up my body in the chair and look directly into his eyes. I try my best to display an innocent expression.

I say in an even voice, "Truthfully, I am being truthful here. It's like this. There was this man. He stopped me on the street corner and offered me five percent of what I take in to sell sausages for him. I didn't know it was against the law."

I slowly lean forward and carefully place my right hand underneath my jacket collar. I have a small hidden pocket there with some rolled-up money. I slowly remove the money from the pocket and place it on the table in front of him. I wipe my sweaty hands on my pants and place them down on the edge of the table. How will he respond to the bribe? Is it enough? Will it get me into more trouble?

He wastes no time in taking the money and putting it into the inside pocket of his jacket. I'm lucky. The bribe works. He hustles me out of the room and walks me towards the building's front door.

He warns me in a loud voice so others can hear. "Don't be so naïve. Next time I will not be so lenient. Don't let me catch you again."

I make a quick exit and inhale the fresh cold air. It's not safe to linger. I reach Leopoldynow by horse and wagon with my life intact but with no sausages or money.

It's three months since my brothers and I have been on the run. Twice I have been arrested, and the prospect of being put in jail, or worse, has hung over me. I tell myself I must stop and think before acting on my ideas to raise money for the farm. No more can I be the same easygoing Jozek living in my home, laughing with friends, and earning money as a furrier. Next time I may not be so lucky to escape severe punishment.

Chapter 8

Three Months of Occupation - I Run Like Hell

Jozek

It's December, one month later. My brothers and I are without clothing to survive the brutal winter. This can't go on. We'll freeze to death. One of us has to go home to bring back warm clothing and convince Mamusia and Sabcia to come to Leopoldynow. It's important for them to escape from Krakow while they can. We have to get them out of German-Occupied Poland under control of the Russians. Our family needs to be together.

The Russian officials controlling the area disapprove of the farm's mission of training people in agriculture to go to live in Palestine. We feel it's only a matter of time before the Russians will shut down the farm. My brothers and I need a plan in place on what to do when this happens. Whatever the Russians want from the Jews, it has to be better than what Hitler has in store for us.

We decide that I will be the one to sneak across the borders back to Krakow. I have no qualms about going. I'm anxious to see Mamusia and Sabcia.

The new Soviet-German border closed last month. It's no small task to smuggle myself across the border. Armed Russians patrol one side of the Bug River and armed Germans the other side. The Bug River crosses the San River and is on the side of a forest outside the small town of Rava-Ruska. There is no bridge or any other way to cross the river. German soldiers, with rifles slung over their shoulders, walk with dogs and patrol the grounds. They will not hesitate to shoot.

I leave the farm with several men also anxious to re-enter Krakow. We hide in the forest behind tall bushes and trees for two nights and three days. We try to calculate what paths to take where we can maneuver without being caught. Someone carefully inches forward to scan the area. We look to see when the soldiers rest and there's no movement. Although not many Germans patrol the area, dogs can sniff for kilometers around.

Of Love and Death

Before the men and I slip into the shallow water, we roll up our pants above our knees and stuff our socks into our shoes. We hang the shoes by their tied laces around our necks. Ice-cold water covers my feet and underscores the chill of fear overtaking my body. We walk across the river in slow-ticking time. We're alert to our surroundings, trying to create as little noise as possible. Once out of the water, we walk some distance before we pull down our soaked pants and put on our shoes and socks.

In Krakow, I am startled to see Jews wearing white armbands with the blue Star of David on their arms over outer garments. I stop a Jewish man hurrying by on the street and ask what it means. He says the armband must be worn by Jews twelve years and older. I am frightened to be without one. I keep my head bent down and try to blend in with the people around me. I resist any urge to cover my right arm as I rush home.

Thankfully the trip is uneventful. A lump appears in my throat when I approach our apartment building. Once I'm inside our apartment, I feel a relief to be with Mamusia and Sabcia. My tears of rejoicing flow as readily as theirs. We hold onto each other, happy we're alive. They want to hear everything about Milek and Manek, about why we couldn't cross the Hungarian border, and our life at the farm. Likewise, I want to know what's happening with them in Krakow.

I plead, "Come back with me. Even though life is not easy at Leopolyynow, it's safer than staying here where we're marked people."

Nothing I say has any impact on my mother. She believes they'll be safe because France and Britain declared war on Germany. Mamusia holds steadfast to that glimmer of hope. I try my best to budge her from her thinking. She's intractable. She's staying. This means Sabcia is staying too.

Life in Krakow has gotten worse for Jews. A wrong word, a stare, or a gesture can bring about immediate detention or imprisonment. In addition to the decree that we must wear the Star of David, Jews are prohibited from going into restaurants, traveling on trains, and worshipping in synagogues. SS, *Schutzstaffelin,* Nazi Party defense and protection squads, drag Jews into the streets and beat them. Nazis are torching synagogues and looting Jewish businesses.

Yet, all this isn't enough for me to sway Mamusia to leave. We decide I will stay in Krakow for several weeks. My hope is that somehow she will see the need to leave with me then. In the meantime, I gather my brothers' and my warmer shoes and bring them to the shoemaker for new leather soles. I sell valuables, such as a silver coffee pot and knickknacks, to pay the shoemaker. Little household money is left. My parents had money for necessities, and more, when my father was alive. That life is gone.

Six weeks later, we say tearful goodbyes. I turn back from the door to plead my case once more. "Mamusia, we should be together," I say with pent-up emotion.

She kisses me on my cheeks and says, "We will be together. Be careful going back to your brothers."

"Don't worry," Sabcia says. "I'll take care of Mamusia. Tell Milek and Manek we pray for the day you can all come home, and we will all be together again."

I hate myself. I've failed. But what more could I have done?

I carry two large suitcases filled with winter clothes and shoes. Daylight has not yet yielded to darkness when I reach the border. Immediately, I find it is more dangerous to cross this time than before. Germans patrol this side of the border in greater numbers. I see and hear the barks of the big black dogs. I train my eyes on the Germans. When I think it is safe, I carefully creep through the forest moving from trees and bushes. I pause each time before I go on. A few feet from the water's edge, I drop myself to the ground and prop up against a large tree. I fight off sleep to wait until the German patrol takes a break, and I can make a run for it.

In the quiet of night, I roll up my pants, stuff the socks into my shoes, and hang the tied laces around my neck. I slip into the water holding the heavy suitcases flat on the top of my head. My arms, neck, and shoulders throb from the weight as I strain to keep the suitcases in place.

I listen for unusual sounds as icy-water sways against my feet. I feel frozen mud cracking as I step gingerly. My teeth chatter. My biggest fear is for the dogs to hear any noise that will alert the Germans. Surely I'll be shot if they catch me. It seems like an eternity but luck is with me. I smuggle myself safely across the river.

January 1940, one month after my initial trip, my brothers and I agonize over the urgency of bringing Mamusia and Sabcia to Leopoldynow. We have no idea what we will do once the Russians force the Akiba organization to shut down this Zionist farm. Milek wants me to make the trip again. I'm anxious to go.

Before I make arrangements to leave, I put on the gold Omega wristwatch my parents gave me on my Bar Mitzvah day. It is my first and only expensive piece of jewelry.

Tatus sits straight in his seat as he listens to me chant Hebrew prayers. I see by his smile and the shaking of his head he is pleased with me, the Bar Mitzvah boy. I stand confident on the bimah wearing the new tallis and yarmulke my parents gave me for my Bar Mitzvah. We celebrate after Shabbos services with a Kiddush in my honor in the synagogue. My family continues the celebration in our apartment. I wrench myself from my memory. I sell the watch for twenty zloty.

It has become treacherous to escape from the Russian border to the German border. I think I am smart.

I hire a Polish farmer, who is recommended to me by a farmer I do business with, to help me cross the river. We depart from Leopoldynow at nightfall. I follow in his footsteps when suddenly, without any warning, he starts to turn back the same way we came.

"What are you doing? Don't leave me. I paid you," I angrily call out to him. He ignores me.

Oh, no. I see the orange flame of his cigarette flaring in the darkness. It will let us be visible for hundreds of feet. The Germans will find me. With my heart racing, I run and hide beneath nearby trees. I try to keep my panic in check telling myself I did it before. I don't need him to help me cross the river.

I crawl and crouch behind trees, tree limbs, and bushes for two days. I wait until I conclude the farmer has left the area. I pay no attention to the sounds of hunger pains, body aches, and rawness of the cold weather. I'm on high alert for anything out of the ordinary.

I move with extreme caution as I make my way to the river. I look for a specific time with a long enough span when the guards halt their walking. I'm patient. When I see a pause, I don't hesitate. I run across the open field toward dense trees and the river. I go down an embankment, hastily roll up my pants, tuck my socks into my shoes and pull the tied laces around my neck.

Once across the icy-cold river, I try to avoid motions or sounds that could attract the dogs. I don't put on my shoes and socks until I'm some distance from the border. Then I run like hell toward Krakow. It's too risky to take a train.

With little money, three zloty, I wind up in a small tavern. Famished, I use all my money and order one dozen scrambled eggs and white bread with butter. I eat it all straight from the frying pan.

It's February of 1940, five months since Krakow was attacked by Germany. I do my utmost to impress upon Mamusia the necessity of her and Sabcia leaving with me. I don't need to expound on the worsening conditions in Krakow and that this isn't a place for Jews anymore. The Germans are slaughtering Jews on the streets. The Polish people hate the Jews. We can't trust anyone.

I explain how the Russians will be shutting down the farm. I beg her to leave so that we can all be together. My voice becomes hoarse. I pace the living room. She's implacable. She points out Leopoldynow is filled to capacity. She still maintains she and Sabcia can manage. She ignores my strong pleas that this will be the last chance to get them out of Krakow.

I look at Sabcia for help. She knows it's a lost cause with Mamusia and shakes her head in agreement with me. My sister dabs her eyes. She's trapped. Sabcia can't leave without our mother. The faded cotton dress on her thin body reflects the growing poverty we are forced to accept. Her once manicured nails are short and unpolished.

By cover of the evening light, I dig up the last of the silver trays in the back of our apartment building. I had buried them there on my last trip back from the farm. I place the trays into a white laundry bag and sling the bag over my shoulder as if it contains dirty linens. The next day I sell them for money for Mamusia and Sabcia to live on.

I feel guilty about leaving without them again. Damn, damn. I don't think Milek could have done any better. Mamusia is in denial. I have a deep sense of foreboding that something terrible is about to happen. I hate to leave them, but I can't stay. I'm afraid for my life.

When I reach the river border, I encounter a dangerous situation. I don't see how I can wade across the river. The Germans have become more adept at border patrol since my last trip. There are more soldiers and dogs. I hear the dogs' growls. It's impossible for me to cross. No option left but to go home. I'm stuck in Krakow.

At twenty-one years of age, I think nothing is too difficult for me to overcome. I used to think I could do anything I wanted, but now I'm a Jew trapped in Poland. I have to wear the armband with the Jewish star. Somehow I manage to earn money so we can survive.

Governor General Hans Frank appointed a *Judenrat*, Jewish Council, comprised of leaders who are important people in Krakow's community. A new order commands every person to work for his daily bread. The *Judenrat* is responsible for the supply of labor for details, such as cleaning streets and toilets, and shoveling snow. Jews are ordered to perform these tasks without pay. We work in street gangs along with Polish workers.

I take my mandatory turn and also substitute for richer Jews. When their turns come up, these Jews pay me to do their dirty work. I give their names instead of mine to the person who checks names off of the list. They're lucky to be rich and not have to do this work. But at least I'm getting money out of this. Sabcia does dirty work cleaning toilets. We have managed to shield Mamusia from doing any work, at least for now.

We live from day-to-day. Danger escalates with more Jews being executed in the streets. We scramble for safety whenever these acts occur. It surprises me that many of the Jews being executed are successful businessmen. I have equated wealth with the privilege of a better chance of survival. I'm shocked to see their positions in life make no difference when it comes to German cruelty.

Germans blame the Jews for the poor economy. They see a few wealthy Jews and a Jewish store on the corner and assume all the Jewish people are rich. It's the wrong assumption. Far too many Jews can barely live on their incomes.

Mamusia, Sabcia and I worry about Milek and Manek. We feel they're safe but only for the time being. We're frightened about what will happen to them when the Russians close down the farm.

But what will Hitler do with the Jews? That is the more urgent question.

Chapter 9

Memory Is Dangerous

Hanka

November 1940, more than a year has passed since Germany attacked Krakow. Governor General Hans Frank has issued a decree that Jews need permits to live in Krakow. Anyone under the age of twelve or over fifty is denied a permit. Roman is seven-years-old.

"What a wasteland," Mamusia says when we arrive at the rented farmhouse in Borek Falecki, a suburb of Krakow.

"Come, Malia, it will be okay," Tatus says helping her climb out of the horse-drawn wagon owned by the Polish driver. Tatus thanks the non-Jewish man he paid in full before leaving Krakow. He puts his arm around Mamusia and walks her into the house.

My brothers and I jump out of the wagon and also thank the young driver. He was polite and didn't say much during the trip. He's the son of a man Tatus knows from when he worked for the Pelikan Pen Company. The driver wishes us good luck as he turns the horse-drawn wagon toward Krakow. I sigh and wish we were headed back with him.

The bone-biting cold rubs up against my skin. The mildew smell strikes a musty greeting when I enter the house. My eyes sweep the large open room with worn country-style furniture: a green sofa, three different chairs covered in cotton with muted colors of brown and yellow, and two tables with glass lamps upon them.

I cast a trail of dusty footprints as I follow Mamusia to the far side of the room used as a kitchen. I sense Mamusia's distress before I see the distaste on her face. It's nothing like the kitchen we left behind. In order to pass by the dark green wooden kitchen table and four chairs, I push a chair aside and see white paint exposed by peeling green paint. Past the kitchen are three bedrooms, one large and two smaller ones. There is no inside bathroom. There's an outhouse.

I wrap a scarf around my head to avoid cobwebs tangling in my hair and help Mamusia clean the farmhouse. When we are done, Mamusia and I put away dishes, clothes, and linens. She stops what she is doing and remembers something she didn't pack, her brown comfortable pair of shoes.

Last summer everyone talked politics. Never did I imagine my family would be forced to leave our home, and we would have to live in this rundown house.

Three days after our arrival, my friend, Marysia, her parents, Mr. and Mrs. Horowitz, and her brother and sister, Henek and Cecylia, come to live with us.

It's crowded, but we go out of our way to get along. To pass time, Roman and I play games of cards and marbles with Marysia, Henek, and Cecylia. My older brother joins us sometimes, but mostly he listens to the BBC on the Blaupunk radio hidden in his closet. It's Manek's and our link to the world. He says he hears nothing encouraging about the war ending soon. The reporting could be wrong. I must hold on to that fact.

Before we were ordered out of Krakow, we lived in constant danger from not only the Germans but also the Polish people. I wouldn't talk to anyone outside my close circle of friends. I never knew whom I could trust. Some of the very people my family and I once had faith in now wear swastikas and are Nazi sympathizers. We are easy targets with the Star of David on our arms identifying us as Jews.

It's deep into winter. We need to go outside to buy food. It takes my brothers a few attempts before they push open the latch on the slanted roof stuck shut from high snow piled up against it. Small blocks of snow fall against our bodies. The three of us put on our snowshoes and go out into the frigid weather to buy milk and bread from Poles living in farmhouses less than a kilometer away. The farmers aren't hostile towards us, but they aren't friendly either. We don't stay after our purchases to talk. Manek says they're afraid to be caught dealing with Jews.

Back at the farmhouse, I wrap my hands around a hot glass of light tea and savor the warmth of the glass as much as the drink. It's awhile before I stop feeling the cold tingling on my face.

Days turn into months, months into spring. Roman and Henek go around the river near the farmhouse to dig up potatoes, pick chestnuts off of the trees, and make fires to burn them on. The boys play soccer using an old can which is wrapped with rags for the ball. The girls and I play hopscotch. When we're not playing, we help with the cleaning, cooking, and setting of the table. There's no more Bronka to do these things. I miss her company.

Food we can't obtain from neighboring farmhouses is not a problem. The Horowitzes are able to get food for us from a grandfather who is a funeral director. Because of his profession he has a permit to move around Krakow. I don't see how he stands it, burying Jews murdered by madmen.

I'm happy. My cousin, Rena Ferber, who is like a younger sister to me, was smuggled out of the ghetto to stay with us but only for a week. Her uncle brought her to the farmhouse and will be back for her. I missed my cousin. She's four years younger than I am. Her father was able to up her age two years on her birth certificate so she could stay in Krakow with her family. Fortunately, Rena's tall for her age.

The golden sun adds color to Rena's pale face. Her dark eyes and dark braids shine as we play outside with the others during the day. Lying in my bed at night, we talk about her collection of Shirley Temple dolls and her David Copperfield novel. She reminds me that my brother Manek taught her to ice skate. We reminisce about me taking her on dates with my boyfriends. She asks about my latest boyfriend back in Krakow. I ask if she has seen him. She hasn't.

The week flies by much too soon, and we hold onto each other with our goodbyes when her uncle comes for her. Mamusia says to let her go, that we'll see her again soon. Will we? Tears drop onto my cheeks as I give Rena a final hug and a kiss.

Life falls into a pattern. But it's getting tiresome doing the same things day after day. I miss the vibrancy of living in Kazimierz with its cafes, movie theaters, and culture. I took it for granted then but not anymore. It was pleasant to live in a place with architecturally grand buildings along the Vistula River. There was an excitement of dressing up and having fun with my friends.

There are so many things I enjoyed that I don't have here. Deep down I know I should be thankful we're not in Krakow under German control, but life here is boring. I feel as if I am suspended on a trapeze swinging back and forth thinking about one life and living another.

Soon after the Germans invaded Poland, the Jewish High Holidays came. The Germans forbid us to go to synagogues and pray. They didn't stop there. It was horrible, shocking, and unbelievable. They destroyed synagogues and burned our holy Torahs and prayer books.

From our apartment balcony, we witnessed the Old Synagogue set on fire. There must have been about one hundred worshippers inside. I clutched Roman's hand as we watched the flames rise. I imagined terrifying images: a pious old man, wrapped in his *tallis* praying to G-d. Fire. Chaos. Trapped. Can't breathe. The old man collapses. Dead.

Barbaric acts abounded in Krakow. From our apartment window, my brothers and I saw the SS drag two Jews into the street and beat them mercilessly. We stood rooted at the window until Mamusia yelled at us to move.

Tatus is not allowed to work at his job as a sales representative for the German Pelikan Pen Company. The company is well known for its fountain pens and stationery supplies. The only money we have to live on is the little money Tatus saved before Germany's invasion into Krakow. He took satisfaction in knowing he could support us in a comfortable lifestyle. Although we were not rich, we lacked nothing. All this has changed. Tatus' weary eyes betray his sad state of mind. He is forced to be without work. Most of his time is spent talking with Mr. Horowitz.

I try not to dwell about my belongings left behind, but I do. Who is going through my drawers, touching my clothes, searching my valuables? I should have thrown my possessions away: books I love to read, photos of family and friends, trinkets I like to wear. I can't stand to think of some Nazi touching my things, sleeping in my bed, living in our home.

Memory is dangerous. I can't let it drag me into despair. When will the war end?

When will we go home? When will we be safe?

Life Before the Holocaust

Rosalia Lipschutz

Abraham Lipschutz

Ferber family (front row: Roman; second row, from left: Malia, Hanka, Leon; back row: Manek)

Henryk Schnitzer with his son Wilus

Frania Schnitzer with her son Wilus

Confinement

Chapter 10

I Could Have Been Caught

Jozek

Trapped. Germans are forcing us from our homes. We must move into the converted Podgorze ghetto by March 20, 1941. The decree for the move is plastered all over Krakow, on buildings' walls, street lamps, and storefronts.

Podgorze is a poor section located outside of Krakow on the right bank of the Vistula River opposite Kazimierz. Polish workmen are bricking up the walls facing the trolley line. Barbed-wire fences enclose the ghetto. Non-Jews living in Podgorze are being transferred to our homes. The Germans are setting up Jewish areas of confinement throughout Poland.

As if things couldn't get any worse, the decree lists items we are allowed to take into the ghetto. The non-Jewish superintendent of our apartment building will check to see that we adhere to the permitted list of our personal belongings. For instance, we can bring no more than one sheet and two pillowcases into the ghetto. One set of linens for three people. What stupid person thought this up? It's absolute madness.

I will not go along with this decree. I have to do something. I tell Mamusia and Sabcia I'm going to smuggle an extra set of linens into the ghetto. I won't let the Germans dictate every aspect of my life. Damn them, damn them all.

Mamusia is scared and tells me it's too risky. She doesn't want me to get caught. To quiet her fears, I tell her I'll think about it, but I've already decided. I must do this. I need to have some control over my life. Who knows what other orders the Germans will demand.

With the sky darkened by night and Mamusia and Sabcia asleep, I remove a white sheet and two matching pillowcases from the top shelf of the hallway closet. I stuff the sheet and one pillowcase into the other pillowcase and tie it like a sack. I go to the kitchen window and lift it open as far as it can go. Cold air smacks my face as I scan the outside area. I search for lights in the apartment building across the way. None are visible.

Now is the time to stop if I'm not going to follow through. I need to do this. It's important for me to feel as if I'm my own person. I reach over the windowsill and concentrate on the ground across the street near the apartment building. I wind my right hand in an arc and hurl the sack. My athletic skill pays off. I hit the target. The linens go the distance near the side of the building.

Instead of ringing for the elevator lift, I discretely tread lightly on the flights of stairs. Once I reach ground level, I stop to listen for sounds. I'm met with silence. Even though I think the superintendent is asleep, I take no chances. I crouch past his apartment so he can't see me. He has an irritating habit of peering out of the top glass section of his door and stopping anyone who carries anything. Then he takes his time examining whatever they have. It's degrading.

Standing outside close to the door and adjusting my eyes to the darkness, I survey the area to see if anyone is in sight. I take my time until I'm confident there is no movement. Then I sprint to the spot where I had thrown the sack and flatten my back against the wall. I keep to the dark shadows on the pavement, out of the light cast by a streetlamp. I'm okay. There's no one here.

I pick up the sack and give it a strong throw to the nearby school grounds. It lands on cement. I run to the grounds and throw it to a grassy area behind the school. A quick scan of the area shows two large bushes. I hide the linens behind them.

Adrenaline pumping, I backtrack the way I came. I lean against the building across from mine and look around for anyone who might be out. All is clear. I speed across the street to my apartment building. I carefully open and close the door, take off my shoes, and tiptoe past the superintendent's door.

I ascend the steps to the third floor under the glow of an overhead black metal light fixture. My pounding heart keeps rhythm with my feet. I could have been caught, could have been caught, but I wasn't. I repeat these words to myself as my socks slide against the linoleum covered steps.

I drop into bed with my clothes on, exhilarated but drained of energy. Sleep escapes me. I toss and turn until daybreak. Where is G-d?

At eight a.m. the next day, four days before the deadline to move into the ghetto, we load a two-wheeled wooden pushcart with boxes and suitcases. As allowed by the list, and checked by the superintendent, we take clothing, pots, dishes, and other limited necessities to set up house in our new quarters.

After tightening the rope to secure the boxes and suitcases to the wagon, I announce we are ready to leave.

"We're never coming back," Sabcia says with conviction.

Giving her a hug, Mamusia says, "It's only temporary."

"Listen to Mamusia. Stay positive," I say. But in my mind I'm thinking, *Sabcia is right. We are not coming back.*

I tell them to put their knapsacks full of additional clothing onto the cart. They insist they're not heavy to carry. Before we start walking, I tell Mamusia and Sabcia how I hid the linens and my plan for retrieving them. Although Mamusia was upset with me before, now she is ready to do what I ask. Sabcia starts to yell her approval but clamps her hands over her mouth.

We start walking in an orderly fashion with other Jews from Krakow. Mamusia waves to a few people. Sabcia clutches her knapsack with both hands and focuses her eyes straight ahead. I know she's bracing herself for what is to come in the ghetto. There are Jews with larger pushcarts than ours. Their carts are filled with boxes and with mattresses hanging out of the sides. Mothers carry babies or grip children by their hands.

My body tenses when I approach the school grounds. Anyone who sees me stop thinks I'm tightening the ropes around the boxes. In reality, I actually loosen the ropes. This is Mamusia's and Sabcia's signal to stand by the cart and shield me.

When no one is walking close by, I slowly topple the cart. Mamusia and Sabcia gingerly pick up suitcases and boxes while I rush behind the bushes, grab the stuffed pillowcase and quickly shove it into a box Sabcia has opened.

Nonchalantly, I reclose the box and tie the ropes around the boxes. I check to see they are securely placed on the pushcart. For a few seconds I savor my victory while my muscles relax. Mamusia and Sabcia do a little skip beside the cart. The thought of winning one over the Germans with this rebellious act soon vanishes as I pull the cart near the ghetto entrance.

Straight ahead is the ghetto wall. It resembles Jewish tombstones placed close together. Why tombstones? Is this a warning foreshadowing our death? Above the gate it says, "Jewish residential area," in German, but the writing is rendered in Yiddish script. German soldiers and Polish police guard the ghetto's entrance.

We sign in with a representative of the *Judenrat* Housing Office at the main entrance. Fortunately for us, the *Judenrat* who is responsible for allocating living quarters gives us a good housing assignment. As luck would have it, I know someone who is on the committee. We are assigned a second floor two-room apartment with a bathroom. Another apartment is situated on the other side of the floor.

Our assigned apartment has a kitchen and a one-room living room-bedroom combination. According to German regulations, flats should be assigned to four families. It's a good sign to have our own apartment. But it doesn't take away the distaste of the apartment's location in this dilapidated area or the dread of leaving our home.

"Phew. What's that smell?" Sabcia asks when she opens the creaky door.

"Burnt boiled cabbage," Mamusia answers wearily placing her knapsack on the sagging gray couch.

Faded yellow paint covers the walls. Nails protrude where things once hung. I bet the non-Jews who lived here didn't have a superintendent tell them what they could take with them.

White curtains frame two small windows. Next to the main room is the kitchen. There is a dark round wooden table with four matching chairs. Against the wall is an empty icebox to keep food cold. The room has a two-gas burner stove and a coal-burning oven.

The couch in the main room pulls out into a bed. There are two large worn chairs. A dark wooden round table and a chipped glass lamp with no lampshade or light bulb are placed between the chairs. I shake my head in frustration. They took the light bulb. Floors throughout the two rooms are covered in a dull brown wood-finish.

Sabcia shivers as she stands in the middle of the apartment. "Are you okay?" I ask her.

"These rooms look so cold. Who lived here? Who's living in our apartment?"

"Don't think about them. For the time being, we should concentrate on life here."

My sister pulls out a silver-framed family photograph from her knapsack. I take it from her. I remember this day. It was my seventeenth birthday.

It was a typically cold first day of November. We posed, grouped in our warm coats and jackets, in front of our apartment building. The photo shows Tatus had one arm around Mamusia and one hand on my shoulder. I stood in front of him. I remember he said I was getting taller. Sabcia stood next to me on the right. Milek and Manek were on my left squeezing into me. The photographer told them to stop joking around. Tatus was dressed in his coat, composed of warm wool on the outside. His coat had a fish otter fur lining and a broad-fur collar. Mamusia wore a navy-blue wool coat. My brothers, sister, and I had on our winter jackets.

I push away the image of our apartment in Krakow. I can't let myself dwell on happier times. Although we are close in distance to Kazimierz, we are living in a world apart.

Mamusia calls for me to bring the box of dishes into the kitchen area. I hand the framed photo back to Sabcia. Mamusia is standing on a chair cleaning out the cabinets. I reach up and hand her dishes and glasses. We use different dishes to keep meat and dairy foods separate.

"Jozek, where will you sleep?" Sabcia calls from the main room.

"I can move the two chairs and sleep on blankets with a pillow."

"That's terrible."

"No other choice."

Chapter 11

The Enemy Will Live Outside

Frania

Loud speakers blast from trucks as they go up and down streets outside our apartment building. "… Jews are commanded to report across the river to the suburb of Podgorze by March 20, 1941."

"Push more to the right Frania." In an act of defiance, we push the storage closet against Wilus' bedroom door.

"There, done," Henryk says. "Those filthy Germans won't easily find the door. Even if they do, they'll have to push this heavy piece of furniture to open it."

"Will we be back?" No matter what he says, I feel in my heart we won't.

"Yes. Yes, I'm sure of it. Come. We need to go."

I stop abruptly before the three of us exit through the doorway. I have a sudden desire to take one last look. I can't believe this has happened, being forced to move out of our home.

"Henryk, wait one more minute. I want to make sure we didn't forget anything."

"Frania, you checked before."

"I won't be long." Before he can say another word, I walk away into the living room. I glance around and rest my eyes on Henryk's favorite place to sit, his rocking chair. I step into the kitchen. The clock above the refrigerator shows seven-forty a.m. Maybe we should have packed the clock. I straighten the three chairs around the kitchen table and take one last look around before I leave.

I enter our bedroom and spread my fingers through the white quilted spread. I couldn't decide between the white or dark blue spread. Henryk said to get the white. I'm glad I did. It gives the room a soothing look. But what difference does it make? The bedroom is not ours any more. Everything seems surreal. I move the small white porcelain bowl and wipe away a spec of dust on the night table with my hand. Will we ever be happy and carefree again?

In the foyer, Wilus tugs on the ear of his stuffed *krolick*. He's too serious. I'm glad we celebrated his fifth birthday earlier this month. His eyes lit up when he blew out the candles. I baked the cake with saved up flour. Henryk's face, normally lined with worry, relaxed and let Wilus' delight wash over him too. We needed that family time of normalcy.

We wait for the elevator lift to reach our floor. Henryk loaded our pushcart earlier. From the front of our apartment building, we see others in the process of putting their belongings onto carts. I have a premonition that nothing good awaits us in the ghetto.

I notice my girlfriend Ania walking out of our building while Henryk is straightening up our sealed boxes.

"Henryk, I'll be right back."

"What now?" Henryk's forehead wrinkles into a frown.

"There's Ania. I want to say goodbye."

"You said goodbye the other day. Make it short."

I take Wilus' hand, as he clutches his toy in his other hand, and rush with him over to Ania. She kneels down to his level, "How are the birthday boy and his *krolick*?"

"I like to play with *krolick*."

Ania hugs Wilus, kisses him, and stands up. She whispers into my ear, "I'm frightened."

I nod my head in agreement and whisper back, "I'm terrified of what lies ahead."

Behind our backs an elderly man speaks loudly to a woman. "It will be good. The ghetto will keep Jews together. The enemy will live outside."

Ania and I look at each other and shake our heads in disagreement with the man's remarks. Good, what's good about being forced out of our homes? I'll miss living here. She embraces Wilus and me again as we say our goodbyes with promises to see each other again soon.

Henryk, waiting by the pushcart, is pacing in place. "Ready now Frania?"

"Yes. I'm ready."

We move on in the street packed with wooden carts. Chatter surrounds us. Neighbors, families, and friends wave to one another. Wilus and I walk behind Henryk at the back of our cart. Wilus is quiet. I squeeze his hand.

"You'll see, Wilus, things will be okay. It will be fun to have a new place to live. Think of our moving as an adventure."

"Will I have my friends to play with?"

"Yes, and you will have new friends too."

"My soccer friends?"

"Maybe, I think so, and do not worry, Wilus, you will have friends."

"Will my bedroom have a light?"

"Yes, it will definitely have a light. You will like your new bedroom."

I try engaging him in conversation along the way, but he's hardly responsive. He doesn't seem to be taking in the people walking around us. He's into himself.

My son has lost his baby looks. He looks cute in his tan pants, a green sweater over a yellow shirt, and a brown jacket with a matching cap. I must make this move fun for him. I don't want my stress to filter down to him. He deserves to be happy.

German decrees made life unbearable in Krakow. Henryk could not work in his tailor shop. He was assigned with other Jews to do manual work, like shoveling snow and cleaning toilets. Our bank account is frozen. Schools are closed. Wilus still has a year before he starts school. I pray to G-d the war will end by then.

The Germans ordered us to surrender our radios, jewelry, and furs. I had to give up the fox jacket Henryk had made for me. I loved the snug feel of the fur wrapping itself around my body. I felt so beautiful when I wore it.

I try ridding myself of the unpleasant thoughts cluttering my mind. *Will we have enough food to eat? It's an industrial section. The apartment will be old.* The walk to the ghetto, with the sounds of voices floating in the air, does nothing to allay my fears.

Henryk stops pulling the cart to ask us, "Are you okay?"

"We're fine, aren't we, Wilus."

"Yes, Mamusia."

My eyes sprout tears that come so easily to me these days. I look at my jacket sleeve, at the hateful white armband with the blue Star of David. I mustn't cry.

Chapter 12

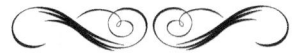

Hiding Means Survival

Hanka

A new edict was issued on March 3rd. We were forced to resettle from the farmhouse to the Podgorze ghetto by March 20, 1941.

We are lucky. My uncle arranged for the Horowitz family and my family to live together in a second floor apartment. The apartment has one centrally located large-size room, with a stove, an icebox, kitchen table and chairs, and two bedrooms. Our bedroom has two beds, one double, one twin, and a sofa. I sleep on the sofa. There is one bathroom in the apartment for both families to use.

One of my uncles owns a house in the ghetto area. Our grandparents live in an apartment on the top floor.

Podgorze doesn't have the Jewish religious, cultural, and intellectual life of Kazimierz. I don't feel as alive. I lack the freedom to do what I want. I feel suffocated by the crush of people relocated to the ghetto. Other Jews forced out of their homes from towns and villages, not just Krakow, are here too.

There's the *apotheke*, pharmacy, the only non-Jewish business allowed in the ghetto. The owner, Tadeusz Pankiewicz, is a Roman Catholic. I hear he persuaded the Germans to let him keep his "Under the Eagle Pharmacy" open on Zgody Square by giving out bribes. He resides in the ghetto and lives above the shop. He could have relocated to the non-Jewish side of Podgorze, but he didn't. His staff comes and goes from the ghetto. Thank G-d Mr. Pankiewicz cares about Jews.

There is a post office, but to whom should I write? My Jewish friends are confined here. As for my non-Jewish Polish friends, I doubt very much they're still my friends. I can't distinguish between a former non-Jewish friend and one who is a Nazi sympathizer now. Even if there were someone to write to, who is to say my letter would get through the mail system. Streetcars travel through Podgorze but don't make stops. We are completely isolated from the outside world.

When my family and I first came to Podgorze, we thought the war would be ending soon. These thoughts are no longer in my mind. We're stuck in this place with no idea of when we will get out.

The *Arbeitseinsutz*, Labor Office, issued my brother, Manek, a *Blauschein*, a document added to his ID, identity card. The *Blauschein* gives him authorization to leave the ghetto and work for a German-run factory. I tell Manek I want to find a way to get out of the ghetto. I'm trapped, like a balloon with its air sucked out. He warns me that even if I could get out, what would I say to get back into the ghetto. I don't have the *Blauschein* to protect me.

It's not safe for Roman and me to play outside. The Germans force Jews to do dirty work. At first, it was mainly the Jewish policemen inside the ghetto enforcing orders from the SS police, but now more of the Germans are moving around the area.

Manek alerts our family when the Germans plan to take an *Aktion* against the Jews. He's fortunate to get advance information from a Jewish policeman who is on the fringe of authority. I questioned Manek about who his source is, even naming people, but he won't divulge the person's identity. He promised to keep the person's name secret.

My brother, Manek, is a realist and a skilled manipulator. He instills in Roman and me that hiding means survival. Mamusia and Tatus remain in the apartment, and Manek runs with Roman and me when an *Aktion* is scheduled. We hurry towards a sewer to hide. Roman runs fast for a nine-year-old boy. Manek pulls open the metal manhole cover. We climb down the metal ladder and squeeze ourselves into the dark sewer. We stand on a ledge with our backs pressed against the cold, wet, rough stonewall.

The stench is awful. The air is charged with stink. Rats and human excretion float by beneath us. Our bodies are cold and clammy to the touch. The dim light casts shadows. Contaminated water splashes onto the ledge and over our legs. I gag and almost throw up. We're not alone. Other children hide here too. We talk in whispers.

"Quiet," someone cautions. "German squeaky boots."

"Gunshots, on top of us," Manek counsels. "Germans are shooting Jews moving out of the sewer. Everyone stay calm."

I stare down at the foul water mixing with human blood and turning the water red. I choke back a shriek.

The next day, when there is quiet from the outside, a boy closest to the manhole cover cautiously pushes it up with his hands. He pokes his head out and tells us the area is clear of Germans.

Filthy, stinky, and hungry, we make our way to our apartment. I take great pains to try to get rid of the noxious smells that envelop my body. I scrub myself over and over and over again.

Another time Manek, forewarned about an *Aktion*, hustles Roman and me to safety out of our apartment into an apartment building that was already searched by Germans. This is much better than hiding in the sewers with the rats and human waste.

Our fear escalates each time we try to become invisible to the Germans. We live in constant dread of running on a moment's notice to escape from them. My brothers and I have become quite adept at this. I hate to think what will happen to us if we ever get caught.

Chapter 13

1942 - She Is Not Me

Frania

Soldiers guard the sealed high walls and gates isolating us from other people. We are prevented from living normal lives. Jews are compelled to live within designated areas marked with a brick fence having wooden markers. We can walk only on certain streets and have an eight o'clock curfew. Rules have tightened. Radios and newspapers are forbidden, although some are smuggled into the ghetto. We have no synagogues or Jewish schools.

Wilus would have started school this year. He's eager to learn. I teach him to read Polish with the few children's books I packed for him.

Wilus clings to me and follows me around. He doesn't ask about his friends anymore. This is not the life for a child to experience. It's not the way I want to raise my child.

Wilus didn't want Henryk to read to him before he went to bed last night. I asked him what he was thinking. "I want to go home. I don't like it here. You and Tatus are sad," he whimpered. I hugged him and proposed he should think about all the nice things he would be doing once we returned home.

He's a sweet-natured child. I love him so much. I need to redouble my efforts not to show my true feelings around him. I have to remind Henryk to do the same.

We share our apartment with two other couples. They have no children of their own and have taken a liking to Wilus. We try to give each other space. The close quarters of a main room, three bedrooms, and one bathroom leave little room for privacy.

Non-Jewish people who lived in this apartment moved out and live in Jewish homes in Krakow. Wouldn't it be ironic if they lived in our home?

Jews who already have homes here in the ghetto are forced to take in additional families. It's a deplorable situation, and one I could never have imagined would happen.

My parents and Henryk's father live in crowded apartments with other families several blocks away.

Henryk's revered mother passed away before the German invasion. We try visiting our parents to reassure ourselves we are all okay. Wilus looks forward to these outings. His grandparents fuss over him. I hate to end these visits, but the Germans patrol the streets. They could beat or kill us for no reason.

I look at my reflection in my favorite hand mirror, a gift from Henryk. The mirror is framed on the front and back with a cream-color flower pattern. The woman who stares back at me is an image of someone else.

She is aged beyond her thirty-three years. She is not me who worked in a millinery shop before my marriage to Henryk. I had a flair for creating fashionable hats. I liked to express myself by decorating them with feathers and beads.

My brown eyes are drained of happiness. My face reveals an unhealthy dull pallor. My smile has faded.

Is that a gray hair showing close to my ear? I pull the strand of hair out. Try as I might for Wilus' sake, laughter has left my life.

My husband appears older than his thirty-five-years. Frowns form in the creases of his forehead. His hair has begun to thin. He has lost his excitement of working in the shop, of preparing for the next project, of making women look beautiful in their custom suits.

Henryk is assigned to work in the Madritsch clothing factory and sews German army uniforms. His workday starts in the early morning and doesn't end until late at night.

We are prisoners within these ghetto walls. Nazis patrol the streets with pistols. Worse yet, we are living a sentence that has no end in sight.

I miss the everyday simple things in Krakow that I once took for granted. I miss the aroma of fresh smells of *chalka*, a sweet white wheat bread, drifting up to our balcony from the bakery. I miss taking Wilus to play in the park. I miss the freedom of shopping for food in my favorite stores.

The *Judenrat* issues a food card to families for use in the ghetto stores. Each person receives a quota of ration coupons. The cards with the coupons contain postage-like stamps you rip off to give in exchange for items like bread, potatoes, and sugar. Jews are not allowed to receive eggs or milk. I stand in line for hours to redeem our coupons. There's a shortage of food and the quality is poor.

We see Jews chopping up their furniture in the streets for fuel. It's a common occurrence, something we haven't had to do yet.

The Nazis invaded the Soviet Union in June of last year. I never imagined the war would last this long. In less than three years, our lives have become a living nightmare.

I want an end to our plight. My hopes and dreams have been shattered. Krakow and I will never be the same again.

Chapter 14

Take Him Away

Jozek

One year of forced labor, constant hunger, and a precarious existence has passed since we entered Podgorze. I am faced with the harrowing truth. We're stuck in the ghetto.

I crave to be free. I want to be the one to control my comings and goings. This is a life I could never have imagined.

We continue to believe that Milek and Manek are safe. It's agonizing not to know if Akiba still manages the farm or if the Russians have shut it down. If they're not at the farm, where are my brothers hiding?

German soldiers and Polish police stand guard outside the ghetto. The Labor Office, controlled by the *Judenrat*, assigns specific work or job assignments, without pay. Our lives are not our own. We're forced to live by their rules.

I have a *Blauschein*, a pass that gets me in and out of the ghetto to my assignment in a furrier shop. The blue card designates me as an essential worker. I repair battle-torn, heavy lambskin wool coats. I also construct fur coats for the SS who plan to take vacations with their wives, mistresses, or girlfriends. Sabcia also has a *Blauschein*. She labors in a clothing factory sewing dresses for German women.

One day in late April, a Jewish policeman stops me and takes me aside when I re-enter Podgorze after my work assignment. He tells me my brother Manek is outside of the ghetto.

"Milek, my other brother, is he with him?" I ask dreading the worse.

"Don't know. No one said anything about another brother."

All the policeman knows is that Manek is in the closest bar outside of Podgorze. He says the Ukrainian guard who smuggled him here wants a reward of five hundred zloty.

The Jewish policeman asks if I have the money. I tell him no, but I will sell my father's fish otter coat. My father's coat, warm wool on the outside with a fish otter fur lining and broad-fur collar, is worth money. I have held onto it for such an emergency.

"Be quick," the policeman cautions me. "I'm told the guard is not one to be kept waiting."

The Jewish policeman walks a slippery slope. He's a good man. He does what he can for us Jews inside the ghetto, but at the same time he must follow exact German orders without delay. The *Judenrat* has the authority to organize the Jewish police, but the police are under the authority of the Nazi occupiers.

The pounding strikes hard against my chest when I take leave of the Jewish policeman. My brain scrambles to make sense of Manek here without Milek. I try to shake off my worse thoughts. *Milek is imprisoned. Dead. No, impossible. He can't be dead.*

I burst into our apartment and blurt out to Mamusia and Sabcia that Manek is at a bar outside of the ghetto. I tell them I need to sell Tatus' fish otter coat to pay the Ukrainian guard who transported him here. Almost in unison, they ask about Milek.

"Manek will tell us. There has to be a good reason he's not with Milek," I say trying to quiet their unacknowledged fears.

I speed out of the apartment with the coat. The happiness of my seeing Manek and bringing him into the ghetto floats in my mind, along with the worry of where's Milek?

A black market for goods exists in the ghetto. I negotiate a good price for my father's coat, six hundred zlotys. This will leave me with one hundred zlotys after I pay off the guard.

I show my work pass for permission to exit the ghetto gate. I walk past apartment buildings in need of paint and repair as I hurry to the neighborhood bar.

Manek here without Milek makes no sense. Something must be wrong. No, it could be all right. Milek could be coming later. I need to get identification papers for them for the ghetto.

War is bloody hell. I feel like a truck stuck in mud, rocking back and forth, sinking further and further into a big hole.

"Hey, watch where you're going!" a man shouts at me when I accidentally step in his way.

"*Przepraszam.*" Sorry. I hang my head and walk away.

My heart is pounding as I reach the bar. I adjust my eyes to the dimly lit narrow room. I observe it's an old but well-kept bar. A jovial bartender pours drinks across the room from the door. A few elderly men with mugs of *piwo*, beer, in front of them sit on bar stools laughing, a rarity in my world. A large poster of Hitler hangs behind the bar. The air is thick with smoke from *papieros*, cigarettes. I look around with the help of a bare overhead light bulb hanging from above.

I catch sight of a young man and a Ukrainian guard sitting at a smoke-veiled table in a corner of the room. A glass mug of *piwo* is on the table. A glass holder with a lit small white candle in the middle of the table casts light on their faces.

The worn tan cotton shirt hangs on Manek's arms and shoulders. His body sinks in his chair. I cross the room in large strides and stand before them.

"Manek."

"Jozek." He stands up and we hold onto each other. "Mamusia and Sabcia..."

"Fine," I interrupt. "Where's Milek?"

He frees his arm and hesitates. Damn, I know what he's going to say.

"Dead," he says quietly.

"No, no. Can't be true."

"I brought your brother from Russia. You owe me money," the guard demands.

The guard's cheeks are flushed with anger. Any fear I might have of the guard is overcome by my grief in learning of Milek's death. I pull Manek down, and we sit across from the guard.

"What happened to Milek?" I face my brother with my question.

"Killed by Germans."

"Where?"

"Kiev."

"Kiev?"

"When the Russians closed Leopoldynow, Milek and I fled to Lvov. We spent over a month there until Germans started to come and round up the Jews. We escaped to Kiev."

"We thought you were safe, if not at the farm, hiding somewhere."

"Enough of this talk! Pay me now, or I will turn your brother over to the German authorities. Russians hate Zionists and so do I!"

The hostile guard explodes. He slams the table with his fist and shakes the mug. *Piwo* splatters on the candle sending off flickers of flames. The bartender and men at the bar turn our way. The last thing I want is their attention.

"Wait, wait. I have the money." I get up, reach into my pants pocket, and unroll five bills. "It's all there, five hundred zloty."

"Give it to me." He grabs the bills and shoves the money into his pants pocket. He stands, grips my arm, and pushes me so that I almost lose my balance.

"Go, take him away."

I turn Manek's shoulder and lead him to the exit. Behind us the Ukrainian guard calls to the bartender for more *piwo*.

We walk fast. "Damn, it's good to see you," I say.

"How do we tell Mamusia and Sabcia?" he asks.

"No way we can hide it from them."

"Milek and I made plans. We were going to escape the Germans and get all of you to safety. We needed more time to work it out, but there were too many soldiers with dogs."

"That's why I never made it back to Leopoldynow. I couldn't figure out a way to get past the soldiers and dogs prowling the grounds. I got as far as the border but couldn't find a way to cross. I failed again to convince Mamusia. I was coming back without them."

"We figured you had a problem crossing the border when you didn't return. We hoped Mamusia and Sabcia would be leaving with you."

Manek and I reach the Podgorze ghetto. Security is tight. You need a pass to get in and out, but we should be okay. I know the Jewish policeman guarding the ghetto gate.

I show my pass to the Jewish policeman. He lets Manek enter through the gate with no problem.

Mamusia and Sabcia run to embrace him as soon as we enter our apartment. Mamusia holds Manek at arm's length and tells him he's too thin.

"Why did you come to Podgorze without Milek? When will Milek be coming? You see we are imprisoned behind the ghetto walls. But it's time for us all to be together."

Mamusia is stalling. She's afraid to hear the truth. Manek clears his throat and evades looking into her face.

"Did they close the farm down, and he wants us to come back with you? You see we can't now. We're prisoners. I guess I should have listened to Jozek and gone to the farm. Jozek couldn't make the trip the last time he tried, so we couldn't have escaped from Krakow anyway."

My brother tries to speak. His emotions take over and he starts to cry. He covers his eyes with his hands and tries to regain his composure.

I am standing close to Sabcia, my eyes watering because of what will come next.

"Manek, what is it my son? Tell me," Mamusia says.

He hesitates and in a rush of more tears, he says, "He's dead."

"Oh, my G-d! No!" Sabcia cries out. "Not Milek."

I grab my sister as her knees buckle and place her on the sofa.

"Get some water and a wet towel," Mamusia orders me through her sobs.

After Sabcia takes a sip of the water and applies the wet towel to her forehead, her color returns. Mamusia's face is streaked with gushes of tears. Manek holds her tight and tries to console her. I can't speak. I have a lump in my throat. Milek was a good brother. I admired him and looked up to him.

Manek tells them what happened. "Milek died in Kiev, killed by German soldiers."

"He was a good boy," Mamusia moans holding onto Sabcia's hand. "Smart, he could have become anything he put his mind to. Remember how he built the crystal radio?"

"Yes," I agree, my body trembling.

"Our goal was to get you back to the farm. Milek and I wanted all of us to be together," Manek says.

My body is contorted with sharp flashes of stomach-knotting pain. No G-d would let Milek die.

"We must say Kaddish," Mamusia says rising up from the sofa.

There is no synagogue in the ghetto to say the Mourner's Kaddish. Mamusia finds a whittled-down Shabbos candle as she searches through kitchen drawers.

"This will have to do," she says. "It's all I have."

We stand close together, heads covered. Facing east, we recite the memorial prayer for the dead by the used candle's glimmering light. *Yit'gadal v'yit'kadash Sh'mei raba…*

By virtue of being the oldest son, I am now head of the family. My father and Milek are dead. G-d has forsaken us. Our family's safety now depends upon me.

Chapter 15

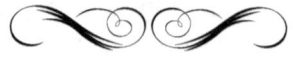

It Is a Match

Jozek

One cannot live in the ghetto without documentation. Manek has none. He has no work assignment. The Germans separate people by the importance of their job. With an important job, it's likely the Germans won't bother with you.

In Krakow before the ghetto existed, I did a favor for a Jewish man I knew from my sports club. I worked in a warehouse and distributed clothing and material to people who had documents to receive specific quantities. This man's wife needed items, such as threads and needles for her millinery store. I gave her two or three times the allotment. The husband appreciated what I did for his wife and told me he owed me a favor. He works in the ghetto. It's his responsibility to give out assignments.

I go to see the husband, and he remembers me. "Don't worry, I will give your brother good documentation papers," he assures me.

True to his word, he creates an identification paper for Manek. He assigns my brother to the Krakow airport labor camp to work in a tailor shop. The airport has been taken over and run by the Luftwaffe. It's a reasonably safe place to work.

Soon after Manek has gotten the airport assignment, I realize my work outside the Podgorze ghetto is no longer safe. I'm frightened by the Germans' heightened *Aktions*. The Germans are murdering Jews outside of the ghetto, rounding up Jews and transporting them out of Krakow to labor camps. I'm terrified that each day I work outside of the Podgorze ghetto, I'm putting my life more at risk.

It's time for me to give up my *Blauschein*. It has given me a misplaced small sense of independence. The pass has given me a chance to get out from behind the ghetto walls, but I'm still a prisoner.

I decide it's critical for me to get an inside labor assignment the SS will view as important. I go back to the same man who helped Manek. I'm fortunate. He assigns me to the airport labor camp as a furrier in the tailor shop. I fix flight packets for the German army. For the time being, Manek and I are safe.

Manek's work at the tailor shop is more important than mine. I can be taken away from my assignment to do odd jobs for the Germans.

One day a trainload of German uniforms, armaments, boots, shoes, anything and everything a soldier may need arrives at the airport and has to be unloaded. The German boss takes several people off of their jobs to help unload the train. I am one of them. Non-Jewish Polish workers who live in Krakow are included in our group. These workers are free to come and go to the airport labor camp.

The day is spent with us unloading the train and carrying the goods on our backs to different warehouses: shoes here, belts there, and pants somewhere else. It's a very large airport base containing many storage areas. At the end of our work time, Jews are transported back by truck to the Podgorze ghetto by a Luftwaffe soldier.

A Luftwaffe soldier transports Jewish workers in a truck from the ghetto back to the airport labor camp the next morning. We sit in the truck bunched together, legs overlapping.

When we arrive at the airport, I go to my place of work. After I report to a German officer, he tells me to go to another office at the airport. My mind spins. *Why? What for?* My stomach tightens with tension. Calm down. It's probably another job.

I enter through a foyer to a large room with several wooden desks. Scattered around the room are wooden chairs, some folded against the wall. German military police are seated at desks. The walls are covered with posters of Hitler. Two military policemen stand near the doorway.

"Excuse me. I was told to report here."

One of the military policemen takes his time looking me over. Then he dismisses me with a wave of his hand and directs me to go to the first desk. I am dismissed as if he's swatting a fly. In another time and place I would have insulted him back, but that was then and this is now.

I stop at the desk of a broad-shouldered German officer sporting a dark mustache and wearing steel-rimmed glasses. I tell him I was sent to report to this office and give him my name. He motions for me to go to the military policeman at the back of the room. I walk up to the military policeman who sits behind his desk, arms stretched behind his head. Above the desk is a map of the ghetto. Fear sharpens my awareness that something is not right. What does he want with me?

"My name is Jozek Lipschutz. I was told to report here."

He has a paper with my name on it. He gets up out of his chair and points for me to stand on a piece of cardboard. The cardboard is laid out on the floor in front of a German officer who carries the rank of major. He is sitting at his desk.

The military policeman tells me to separate my feet. He takes out a pencil and traces my worn brown cracked-leather shoes. Why is he taking an outline of my shoes? I know survival depends on chance incidents. Nothing I can think of remotely relates to an outline of my shoes. What the hell is going on here?

"Wait here," he commands.

Sweat gathers under my armpits and drips down the sides of my body under my shirt. My mind travels all over the place. *What could they want with me? What could I have possibly done?* There's nothing I can think of that makes sense.

Two military policemen take the cardboard I stood on to a room in the back. The major is busy with paperwork at his desk that is covered with piles of neatly arranged folders. I try my best to exhibit a calm presence while my body shivers with fear. I don't have long to wait. They return in a few minutes.

"It is a match!" One of them exclaims with delight to the major.

Match? What match? What do my shoes' outline on the cardboard mean? I filter his words through my brain and cannot come up with a logical explanation.

"Your shoes match the marks on the window of the warehouse," the major says sitting at his desk and pointing a finger at me. "This proves you broke into the warehouse last night and stole two hundred pairs of shoes."

"What? I didn't do that. I couldn't have."

Anger flares my cheeks. A rush of energy overtakes me. Since I speak German quite well, I reply rapidly in his language. "I couldn't have been at the airport at night. Jews are counted when we leave the Podgorze ghetto in the morning and again when we enter the airport gate." My voice takes on a higher pitch. "Also in reverse, we are counted when we leave the airport labor camp after a day's work and counted again when we enter the ghetto."

I lean my palms on the edge of the major's desk to steady myself, almost knocking over some of his folders. "Herr Major, anyone who is pointing his finger at me is doing so because I'm Jewish." I take a deep swallow. "They know anything can be blamed on a Jew." I sense eyes on me from the other Germans in the room. I remove my hands from the major's desk and straighten up my body.

He clicks his shiny black leather boots, jumps up from behind his desk and shouts at me. "I'm here to solve a burglary! I do not play the SS game! If your story checks out, you will be free!"

I don't hesitate. With extra chutzpah I answer him in German, "If you get truthful answers, you will find I did nothing wrong."

He sits his almost six-foot frame behind his desk. He lights up a cigarette and gestures for me to sit in a chair at the right side of his desk. His underling stands directly in front of me, a smug look pasted on his face. According to him, my fate is sealed. All he wants is someone to blame, especially a Jew.

"Get me the guard assigned to the airport gate!" The major yells into his phone.

His cigarette smoke burns my eyes. I hear him question the guard about Jews being counted coming and going to the airport but cannot hear the guard's replies. The major puts down the receiver and turns to face me.

"The guard confirms your story. You're free to go back to your work assignment. I look only for the truth."

I barely get my voice to utter, "Thank you." I am overcome with emotion as I try to slow my breathing. I get up from the chair and hesitate to shake the German's hand.

"Thank you," I say louder and stronger this time as I stand in front of his desk.

Behind me I hear the military policeman say, "But his shoes match." You lousy German, I bet your shoes match too.

"It's not him," the major snaps. "Get me another match."

Damn right. It's not me. It took all of my energy to speak up to the major. I make my way back to my assignment in the tailor shop. I'm alive, alive to live another day.

A few days later, I learn two of the non-Jewish Polish workers were arrested and imprisoned for stealing the shoes. The Polish workers had helped to unload the train and didn't have to be counted as they came and went from the airport.

Lucky for me the major looked at the situation objectively. He's the only German I have encountered who has stuck up for a Jew.

Chapter 16

I Should Have Seen This Coming

Jozek

It's June of 1942. Everyday life continues. I get lucky. My assignment as a furrier at the airport labor camp has become more important. German officers learn I can sew fur slippers and fur gloves for their wives, girlfriends, and mistresses.

One day when Manek and I return to our apartment after our assignments at the airport, we see Mamusia and Sabcia in distress holding onto each other crying. Their faces are drenched with tears.

"What happened?" I ask as Manek and I surround them.

"Mamusia is being deported. She has no identity work card stamp."

"Must be a mistake!" Manek explodes.

"No mistake." Sabcia says leaving hold of Mamusia and taking her handkerchief out to dry her red teary eyes. "We were told to assemble in the plaza. Only those who received work assignments can stay. Mamusia has none. She leaves tomorrow."

"No. She won't go. I won't let her. I will ask the Jewish policeman to remove her from the list," I say.

"Nothing we can do, Jozek. I talked to him. I pleaded with him. He says he's following orders."

"The hell with the orders." I slam my hands together, my mind digesting the horrible news.

Mamusia is not quite fifty-three-years-old. The Germans want to get rid of her because they think she's old. Mamusia is not old, but she is vulnerable. She has no work assignment. Mamusia has no assignment because they would not give her one. Damn those lousy German bastards.

If in the Gestapo's opinion a prisoner cannot contribute to the war effort, the Gestapo will refuse to put a stamp on the identity work card of that prisoner. Anyone who doesn't get his or her identity card stamped is forbidden to remain in the ghetto.

Mamusia sits down on the sofa sobbing. I use my handkerchief to wipe away her tears. I want to scream. I blame myself. I should have seen this coming. What can I do to prevent her from going on the transport? Think. Think of something, I tell myself.

"I'll arrange to go with you," I say.

"No. You must all stay together."

Try as I might, I can't come up with anything that will stop her deportation. Guilt turns to rage. Where is G-d? Why must we Jews always be the ones to suffer? First Milek is murdered. Now Mamusia is to be deported. I'm devastated. My mother is a good person. She would never harm anyone. What will the Germans do to her? Where will she be sent?

Sleep eludes us. We go back and forth from the grim reality of her forced deportation to happier times. We pass the night with talk about when Tatus was alive and his business thriving. We reminisce about Milek and his talent to construct things. Why can't I come up with an idea to save her?

"Mamusia, *Kocham cię*, I love you. Take care of yourself. I have high hopes we will get together when the war will be over," I tell Mamusia before she steps away from our apartment building.

"Mamusia, *Kocham cię*," Manek says and gives her a hug as he squeezes past me.

"Mamusia, I…" Sabcia cries uncontrollably.

In early morning, heartbroken and helpless, we witness Mamusia, along with thousands of men, women, and children, being forced to march by the SS through ghetto streets to the railroad siding. Back in our apartment we hear the outside pounding of the SS' boots. We witness horrific scenes of shots fired at innocent people who can't keep up with the marching pace.

It's inhuman. It's madness. The sounds of the shots, crack, crack, crack and piercing cries of the victims pound against my skull.

Once the SS have left, we join others on the sidewalks and stare at the gruesome sight of hundreds of bodies lying in the streets. Their blood is a red river pouring into gutters. I gag on the pungent odor that smothers the air. The smell whips my body to nausea. The sight has me kneeling on my knees. Mamusia, Mamusia, what will happen to you? G-d where are you? How can you allow this to happen?

I hear a man, standing in the doorway of our apartment building, chanting the Mourner's Kaddish. Getting up, shaking my head in acknowledgement toward him, I join in reciting the prayer for the dead.

Mamusia's whereabouts after she was herded into a cattle car is unknown. A family friend made his way following the line of packed cattle cars as far as he could go without being caught. He couldn't tell where the prisoners were headed because the cattle cars reached a point where the tracks split. Rumors quickly spread throughout the ghetto that the cars were headed to three camps: Belzec, Majdanek, and Treblinka.

We've heard reports that the Germans held a conference in January to discuss plans for murdering all the Jews of Europe. The death plan called for camps to be equipped with gas chambers and special crematoria.

G-d, if there is a G-d, Mamusia will survive. Now without Tatus, Mamusia, and Milek, we are down to a family of three. The life that we exist in shows no mercy. Mustn't think that way about Mamusia. She has to live.

I roll over on my makeshift bed and wait for what morning will bring.

Chapter 17

We Must Survive

Jozek

Smack. A woman hits into the right side of my body. Her bucket and cleaning supplies scatter on the ground. Chocolate brown eyes, highlighted with thick dark brown eyebrows, scrutinize me while I lower my eyes to examine her.

Where other young women's bodies are flat, like dresses hung on a hanger, her petite body embraces curves. Short dark brown hair crops her ears. Natural color dots the full lips of her youthful face.

I extend my hand to her. "Jozek Lipschutz, at your service." *Wow. I'd like to see her again.* Her smile illuminates her face like the flame of a match.

"Hanka Ferber, nice to meet you. Sorry. I didn't see you coming." She points to the building left of us. "I'm in a hurry to get to the officers' apartment building."

I stoop and help her gather up the cleaning bottles and cloths. "I'm blinded by your beauty," I say as she takes hold of the bucket with the supplies.

"My assignment is a furrier. In another world, I would sew you a mink coat." *I know just the style that would show off her beauty.*

She lets out a soft laugh. Her eyes sparkle with friendliness. "Don't forget the matching hat." *He's handsome.*

With no time to waste, I ask her to meet me in the evening at the airport fence. The barbed-wire fence separates the men and women's quarters. Prisoners gather there in the evening.

Those of us assigned to the airport labor camp now live in quarters on the airport compound. Because of a deportation *Aktion* on October 1942, to reduce Podgorze's population, the air force general decided Jewish airport workers should not go back to the ghetto. We are housed on the airport grounds in two barracks, one for men and one for women, with approximately one hundred prisoners in each.

"Okay, I'll be at the fence." *He's reading my mind. I want to see him again.* "I have to go."

"I'll look for you," I say.

Hanka nods her head in agreement and walks away. Our forced labor allows no time for lingering and small talk. We need to be at our assignments. We can't afford to be questioned by Germans seeing us together.

Hanka opens the building's door as I start towards my place of work. I begin with a bounce in my gait but stop to slow down my pace. It's best to be invisible to my surroundings.

I'm glad Sabcia secured a sewing job at the airport labor camp. I don't have to worry about her being deported. She, Manek, and I, and my new acquaintance, Hanka, are safe from selections because of our airport assignments, at least for now.

Hanka and I meet in the October evening, already much cooler than September. *I wish I had a jacket to place around her shoulders. Why do I even have such thoughts? I'm useless to do anything. Can't go back to my life in Krakow.* The barbed-wire fence imposes our separation. *Damn.*

"No samples of mink?" *He's older, mature.*

"None that would grace your beauty. I promise, I'll dress you in mink one day." *Why couldn't I have met her before in my other life, my life in Krakow?*

"That would be wonderful," she says as she wraps her hands around her chest.

I savor my feelings of actually being with a woman. It's nice to hear the comforting ring of her voice. We smile at each other and share our life stories.

I start first. I tell her about my father who died of a stroke in 1936 because anti-Semitism caused him to lose his business. He sold fruit baskets, candy, and canned fish in his store until customers stopped coming.

My voice cracks as I describe my mother, a kind-hearted and loving person. I mention my recurring nightmare where I see her for the last time being marched away by the SS. I share my innermost thoughts that I will Mamusia to be alive. I curse the Germans. She gestures with fingers on her lips not to utter these words. I know she's right. One has to be careful of what is said aloud.

I talk about my brother, Milek, the oldest child in our family. He graduated from a mechanical school after high school and worked as an engineer for a family friend. "Damn, Milek was too good to die. He was killed in Kiev. He and my brother, Manek, escaped from the Zionist farm and wound up in Kiev."

"I'm sorry for your father's death. Your brother's murder is terrible." She hears my pain. She says with conviction, "You will see your mother again. You have to believe this. You must have faith."

"It's difficult." I shove my hands, clenched in anger into my pockets.

"We can't give up."

"I know you are right, but it gets harder and harder. I know I mustn't let my despair crush my will to survive."

I continue to pour out my heart to her about Manek and Sabcia who are assigned to labor at the airport. "Manek was in high school before Germany invaded Poland. Money was tight, but we managed to save for his high school tuition.

"My sister has magic hands and sews beautiful clothes. I believe if Sabcia was given the chance, she could work in the best of the fashion houses."

I reminisce about how we spent ideal summer vacations in the Carpathian Mountains at a camp owned by my aunt. I mention Sundays when my parents hired a horse and buggy for our enjoyment.

"We would go to one of the parks outside of the city where my brothers and I played soccer. Mamusia always prepared food for us to eat during the day."

"You and your family had a good life," she says. "We did too. I miss my friends."

"A pretty girl like you must have lots of friends."

"Thank you. Yes, I do have friends, did have friends – wonderful friends." *I like the way he towers over me.*

"Before the Germans took over, my friends and I would see the latest movies and go to the cafes. We had classes together at school."

She fills me in on her family. "My parents, Malia and Leon Ferber, and my brothers, Roman and Manek, are in the Podgorze ghetto. I'm scared for their safety with the *Aktions* taking place. Tatus tries to maintain a calm demeanor for us, but I know he's distraught. He was always the one who protected us. Now he can't."

I don't interrupt her and let her talk. *I wish I could take away her pain.*

Her face grimaces as she tells in exact detail how she and her brothers hid in the sewers to escape from the Germans. "One wrong step and we could have died." She wrinkles up her nose, "The smell was sickening."

"I'm glad you are alive and that I met you, even though you did try to run me down."

"But I didn't do it on purpose," she says with a laugh.

Good. I got her to laugh. I disclose my birthday is next month. "I'll be twenty-four." I wait for her to say her age. It's obvious she's younger than I am, but we all age in the camp.

"Makes you older by six years."

I sense she is wise beyond her years. I crave female conversation. I miss playing sports with my friends. I miss family dinners. There are so many things I miss that I may never have again.

Being with Hanka feels good, but the barbed-wire fence that divides us is a grim reminder we are not free. We are slave laborers to be used until we drop dead. Somehow we must survive.

I think about Hanka whenever I have a few moments to myself. I envision us at the movies, in cafes, and at the park. I show off my skills at playing soccer and ping-pong. Some day we will do all these things. Keep dreaming. That's all it is.

Another evening, under a darkened threatening sky, we stand across the fence and talk about how difficult life was in Krakow after the invasion and before being expelled to the Podgorze ghetto.

"We weren't allowed to use our telephones. It was amazing," she marvels, "to converse on this new contraption."

It's nice that her family had a telephone. My family could not afford one. All extras were out of our reach when Tatus lost his business.

Other rulings also restricted us from going on with our lives. Jews were forbidden to travel on trolley cars. When we saw soldiers on the sidewalks, we had to walk in the streets.

Our rabbis reasoned the war would not last long. Terror escalated. People who escaped from being caught reported the Germans were taking truckloads of people into the forest and shooting them.

"Before we were forced to move into the ghetto," Hanka says, "we were ordered to leave Krakow because of Governor General Hans Frank's decree that anyone under the age of twelve or over fifty wasn't allowed to stay. We moved to a farmhouse in Borek Falecki, a suburb of Krakow. I can feel the bitter cold when I think about that place. It was an undeveloped wasteland."

"If it bothers you, we can talk about something else."

"No, I'm okay. It wasn't entirely awful. We lived in the farmhouse with the Horowitz family. They were friends of my parents and had kids. We played together. I miss going to high school. I miss learning about foreign places. Places I guess I'll never get …"

"Don't think like that," I interrupt.

"I hope you're right. When we were forced to come to the Podgorze ghetto, we thought the war wouldn't last long. There are times when I wonder if we'll ever get out of here. But then there are other times when I know I will survive. I can do the work. I'm young and strong."

"You are young and strong. You must keep thinking that way."

I tell her how I defied the Germans and smuggled an extra set of linens into the ghetto escaping the scrutiny of the apartment superintendent. I put myself in a bright light when I tell Hanka how I felt compelled to disobey the German order.

"You were brave to take such a big risk."

"I had to do it. I had to feel as if I still had some piece of control over my life."

She says they had lived at the farm for about one year before they were ordered to move into the ghetto with the Krakow Jews. Her family shares their quarters in the ghetto with the Horowitz family.

"That must make things more bearable living with them."

"Yes, it does. When I heard the Germans wanted people to clean out officers' apartment buildings at the airport, I realized it would be a good assignment, safer than working in the ghetto. Work, it's the only thing that keeps us alive."

How right she is. The Germans warn us that work will keep us alive, but they are devious. Every few months there's a new system and the need for another identity card. If you are not issued a new card with a work assignment stamp, as Mamusia wasn't, you are in danger of being transported or killed.

This must not happen to us. We have to preserve our strength. We need to have the strength and will to survive.

Chapter 18

We Are Kept Like Caged Animals

Jozek

In March of 1943, Commandant Reimelt, in charge of the Krakow airport labor camp, commands Jews to be inoculated against some kind of disease. A Jewish doctor gives us the injections.

The inoculation medicine is scarce as are the needles to inject the medicine. The same needle is used over and over and over again. My right leg, above the knee to my thigh, swells like a balloon and keeps swelling from the injection.

The German doctor stationed at the airport refuses to operate on Jewish prisoners. Because of this, the commandant has me transported to a hospital in the Podgorze ghetto for surgery. I have never met the commandant. I'm thankful he cares enough to send me for the surgery. He's a good man.

Before the war, this three-floor hospital was a Polish police station. The Podgorze ghetto hospital is ill equipped. A doctor performs the operation on me under anesthesia. It takes time to complete the surgery on my right thigh. I wake up during the operation and see lots of blood on my leg. There's not enough ether available to use on all the patients. The doctor lands a hard punch to knock me out again.

After the operation, the doctor has no pain-killing medication to give me. I clench my teeth and try not to concentrate on the terrible pain.

I am lying in bed. My leg is bandaged with cloth made out of heavy rags that reaches from my hip to below my knee. Three tubes are inserted into my leg to drain the infection.

I'm lucky. I'm in a bed by myself. Most of the other patients in the ward share their beds with others. I would hate to have another patient in bed with me and have him accidentally kick my leg. I'm assigned a bed for myself because of contacts I have with people who know people in charge of the hospital.

The putrid hospital smells are smothering. What saves me from inhaling the constant stench is that my bed is close to the exit door. Fresh air enters when the door is opened and closed.

A Jewish policeman guards the door of a Jewish prisoner who is in a bed in a separate room in the hospital. Last night the prisoner told the policeman he needed to use the bathroom. While the policeman stood guard at the door, the prisoner escaped through the bathroom window. The bathroom is located next to the exit door near my bed. There was a big commotion in the hospital after it was discovered he had escaped.

Two SS soldiers storm into the ward with revolvers drawn. They look around and stop at my bed. With revolvers pointed at my head, one of them shouts, "You helped the prisoner escape!"

What the hell! They're going to kill me. "No! No! Not me. Look at my leg," I appeal to them. I scramble to pull on the rags on my leg. I want to show the SS soldiers I can't get off of the bed by myself with my heavily bandaged leg.

They're going to pull the triggers. Splashes of perspiration, like a pitcher of water pouring down my back, soak my skin. I don't want to die.

I sense other patients holding their breaths. Frozen in space, I stare at the soldiers. At that exact moment when I am certain they will pull their triggers, someone from outside the hospital calls to them at the door. Just as quickly as they entered, they turn around and leave. I gulp some cool March air escaping from the exit door before it shuts closed. Relief floods through my body. I am alive.

There is no sleep for me at night. I have visions of the SS coming back to the hospital with their revolvers drawn and pointed at me.

Two days later, I'm lucky, the commandant sends a German Air Force soldier with a horse and buggy to take me back to the airport labor camp. I leave the hospital with bandages and tubes still in my thigh feeling lucky to escape from another encounter with the SS soldiers.

Soon after my return to the camp, I learn the doctor in the Podgorze ghetto hospital had the nurse administer hydrocyanic acid mixed in glasses of water to the patients. It was a mercy killing in response to orders to liquidate Podgorze. I wonder if the commandant had advance notice of the mercy killings and speeded up getting me back to the airport.

If I had been there, I could have been one of the patients administered to with the acid. I could have been killed. How many more chances will I have to stay alive?

On March 13, 1943, the Podgorze ghetto liquidation begins. German soldiers armed with rifles force Jews to leave their apartments. Anyone found hiding in an apartment is killed on the spot. Dead bodies line the streets. It's a living hell.

While the ghetto liquidation goes on, Hanka, Manek, Sabcia, and I remain at the airport labor camp. We are not being moved out and are somewhat safe here.

Hanka's parents, Malia and Leon Ferber, her brothers, Manek and Roman, her aunt and uncle, Frania and Henryk Schnitzer, and their son, Wilus, are moved to a newly built concentration camp. The camp, "KL" Konzentrationstagger, is called Plaszow. Located within city limits, it's less than 4 kilometers, 2 miles, east of the Podgorze ghetto. I hear Plaszow was chosen because it's close to the railroad station.

Three months later, June 1943, the Germans take more than half of the Jews out of the airport labor camp to Plaszow. Hanka, Manek, Sabcia, and I are not moved out. So far our jobs are important enough not to be transported to the concentration camp. How long will our luck hold out?

The two prisoners' barracks, separated by a barbed-wire fence, currently have approximately fifty men and fifty women in each one. A barbed-wire gate to the encampment is guarded day and night. We are kept like caged animals.

Transportation of Jewish workers out of the airport labor camp is still taking place. Horrific things are happening. In one instance, I hear tragic news about a Jewish doctor who lives outside of the airport encampment in a small house with his wife and baby son.

The doctor hid his baby during an attack on his home. When the SS entered his house, they found some sign of their baby. The SS searched their home and discovered their son who was hidden in the attic. The entire family was shot on the spot.

I learn from Jewish prisoners that Commandant Reimelt is shocked the family was murdered. I'm told he never thought the Germans would kill the family. Well, now he knows. Who does he think he is dealing with?

December 1943, without any warning to the prison workers, the SS evacuates the Krakow airport labor camp. They round us up, squeeze us into trucks, and transport us to the Plaszow labor camp. Hanka reunites with her parents, brothers, her aunt, uncle, and their young son. Now we are under the command of the murderous *Haupstürmfuhrer*, Commandant, Amon Goeth.

Chapter 19

Plaszow – My Life Could Have Ended in a Stinking Hole

Jozek

Can you imagine ever being completely powerless to have control of your life? I didn't. But that's exactly what has happened to me.

My father died of a broken heart because of the Polish people's hatred of Jews. He lost his business. A business he loved and worked so hard to build. Germany invaded Krakow. My brothers and I escaped to the Leopoldynow Zionist farm. We thought the war would soon end when France and Britain entered the war on the third day. We were wrong.

My brothers and I wanted Mamusia and Sabcia to leave Krakow and come with me to the farm. On my last trip to try to get them out, I became a Jew trapped in Krakow. While Manek and Milek were at Leopoldynow, Mamusia, Sabcia, and I were forced to move to the Podgorze ghetto.

Manek was brought to the ghetto by a Ukrainian guard who wanted a ransom, or he would turn him over to the Nazis. Milek was murdered in Kiev. The Germans denied Mamusia a stamped identity card that would allow her to work. Because of this, she was deported out of the ghetto to where we do not know. Manek, Sabcia, Hanka, and I were assigned to forced labor at the Krakow airport camp.

All these events are beyond any horrors my mind could conjure or anyone should ever endure. Yet as terrifying as life was before, it doesn't compare to my life now in Plaszow under the command of the murderous SS Hauptsturmführer, Amon Goeth.

I witness acts of evil too horrible to comprehend. I see torture and pain inflicted on innocent people. For the first time, I witness the actual resolve to kill. Concentration camp Plaszow is built as a labor camp, but the Germans find the means to murder people all the time.

We are enclosed in the camp by electrified-barbed wire. The watchtowers have machine guns and spotlights. The Germans don't care who sees their murderous acts. They believe no one will live to tell what transpires here.

Commandant Goeth, born in Vienna, is an SS officer in his early thirties. He has turned the camp into a business. He took over command of Plaszow in February of 1943. Goeth has prisoners used as slave labor and assigned to work in various shops. He supplies some goods from these places and others to the SS and wealthy German officials.

Goeth needs no reason to murder people. He's a psychopathic killer, a heavy drinker, and extremely violent. No one wants to be caught in his sight.

One day I'm walking to my assignment, and Goeth is up ahead across from where I'm going. My heart starts to thump when I see him. He is six-feet-four-inches tall. Goeth is riding on a horse and sitting straight on his saddle. I'm frightened of him, and I slow down my pace.

Goeth notices paper on the ground. I'm close enough to hear him yell to a prisoner walking near him, "Pick up the paper!" The prisoner bends down and picks up the paper.

What occurs next belies all matter of reasoning. Goeth fires down at the prisoner. Bang! The prisoner falls to the ground, murdered. Goeth rides away.

I'm immobilized by what I just witnessed. I implore my senses to command my body to walk to my assignment. If I were closer, I would have been the one ordered to pick up the paper. I would have been murdered. Survive. Survive. Survive becomes my main priority. I must not let Goeth and his evil madmen get the best of me.

The path to survival is to be an important part of the German forced-labor strategy. Each prisoner at Plaszow has an assigned number. We are dehumanized and no longer referred to by name. The number imprinted on a ribbon is attached to our jackets. The ribbon has a colored-triangular symbol. The symbol indicates the classification of the prisoner

Jews have two triangles forming a Jewish star. One yellow triangle pointing down indicates a Jew, and one red triangle pointing up denotes a political prisoner. Non-Jewish prisoners' ribbons usually have only one triangle.

A bugle blast at five a.m. starts our day. Prisoners receive a hot black drink, not coffee but ground-roasted grain. At midday, we get this drink with a soup made up with potato peels. I look at the prisoner doling out the soup wanting to make a connection with him, hoping he will put potato peels in my bowl. It rarely happens. A slice of black bread in the evening completes our everyday diet. Some days we get even less.

Hunger pains never cease. One evening I save half of my evening slice of bread to eat with the morning drink. I wrap the bread in my jacket and place the jacket under my head when I go to sleep. I can't stop thinking about the bread under my head. Exhausted and starved, I quickly chew the bread. Even though I still have stomach cramps, I can now fall asleep.

Sleeping arrangements consist of three layers of long narrow wood shelves with a few pieces of straw on the outside walls. Each prisoner is allotted an area of about two feet by six feet.

Toilet facilities are long latrines with a plank on which men sit while defecating. There is a steel pipe about fifty-feet long that hangs horizontally with small holes spaced every couple of feet from which water drips at some unsteady pace. This is our washroom where we are allowed to spend only a few minutes each morning. There are no showers, no laundry facilities.

Around six a.m. we assemble in an open field, the *Appellplatz*, for roll call. We stand in lines to be counted according to our work assignments. German guards, many with dogs, count all the groups and prohibit prisoners to move from their place until the guards have completed the correct count according to their records.

We are dressed in minimum clothing, striped thin cotton uniforms consisting of pants, jacket, and a cap. We have no underwear, no shirt, no socks, or shoes with heavy soles. My wooden shoes, one black and one brown, are different sizes. I organize some rags to wrap around my feet in place of socks.

It's a far cry from when I was dressed in my custom powder-blue suit. *I'll wear it again one day.* Somehow, some way, the hell with the odds, I'll survive.

Rain, snow, freezing cold, does not matter. We're forced to stand in the *Appellplatz*, sometimes for a couple of hours. Only when the count is correct are we marched by groups to our work assignments.

I witness prisoners with no assignments taken to a large field where truckloads of dirt are dumped at one end. They're given a wheelbarrow and told to load the dirt. The prisoners must push the full wheelbarrow quickly to the other end of the field where they unload the dirt.

Prisoners follow each other in a circle. The SS speed them along with their whips. This goes on all day until the dirt is moved to the other end. The next day prisoners perform the same labor but move the dirt back to the original place.

After our day's work, we are marched back to the *Appellplatz* and counted again before we're permitted to go to the barracks for the night. The Germans are obsessed in wanting an exact prisoner count.

In early 1944, I'm ordered with two men to dig holes for machine gunners. The Germans, at war with Russia, are preparing for an attack by the Russian army. We are each given a wheelbarrow, a pick, and a shovel. Plaszow is set on hilly terrain and is very uneven. It's hard laborious work to dig the holes because the ground is full of rocks.

A passing SS officer catches the three of us resting on the wheelbarrows. He shouts at us, "You lazy Jews!"

Then as if I'm watching a slow moving scene out of a movie, the officer puts on his gloves, unsnaps his revolver, and lines us up at the edge of the hole we have just dug. Then he punches each of us so hard, we fall backwards into the hole.

Pain penetrates my left shoulder where he struck me. He motions down with his revolver for us to climb up out of the hole. He punches us once more. We fall back down into the muddy hole. Again, he points the revolver at us. We push our battered sweaty bodies and struggle to climb out of the hole, only to be punched down again and again. Wincing with pain, with the thick mud adhering to our bodies, it takes longer and longer to climb out of the hole.

Eventually the SS officer stops pointing the revolver at us, apparently tired of playing his game. He puts the revolver back into his holster, removes his gloves, and walks away.

I am physically and mentally exhausted from the ordeal. It doesn't sink in until I get back to the barracks at night. My life could have ended in a stinking hole.

In the summer of 1944, the Germans assign me to a group that removes mud from the bottom of a small drained lakebed. The job consists of pushing a wheelbarrow downhill over about one hundred feet of boards about two-feet wide. I load the wheelbarrow with mud and push it uphill over a similar board and dump the mud. We do this for the whole day. If you fall off the board and can't come back up, you are shot on the spot. I force myself to focus on what I am doing as shots ring out and strike at fallen prisoners. Somehow I manage to survive.

Another day on assignment, I take a shovel full of mud to sling into a wheelbarrow. My right leg gives way. I tumble into the lakebed. Mud splatters into my hair and face and drips from my nose. Muddy and slightly bruised on my right side, I climb out of the lakebed and find myself standing across from a German guard, arms folded, legs apart. The guard has been watching me work.

"You fool!" he screams. He pulls his gun out of the holster.

I see the fire in his eyes. He's enjoying this. He aims, his right trigger hand steady. I throw my muddy hands up over my head, and I fall to the ground on my knees. This is it. I am going to die.

Then out of nowhere, a broad-shouldered tall Jewish policeman appears above me. With his back to the German guard, he hits my back with a one-two punch with his powerful large hands. He follows by jerking his head and pounding the air with his left and right fists.

"There, he got his punishment!" he exclaims and turns to face the guard. His words hang in the air like a parachute waiting to open.

"Get up! Up! Get back to work!" the Jewish policeman shouts as he turns back to face me.

I try to steady my trembling body and stand erect. The German guard shrugs at the Jewish policeman, puts his gun back in the holster, and walks away. The policeman heads off in the opposite direction of the guard.

Hands shaking, heart pounding, I straighten the wheelbarrow and start to clear mud from the lakebed. I feel tears, streaked with patches of mud, leaking down my cheeks. I'm afraid to stop working to wipe them away. The tears create a wet mud pie on my face. My legs are covered in mud. I wish I could have thanked the policeman before he left. He saved my life, at least for now.

After these life-threatening assignments, I'm fortunate to be rescued to labor at a somewhat safe job. Hanka's uncle, Wilek Chilowicz, the Jewish Commandant of Plaszow, is responsible for getting me assigned to the fur shop. Better yet, Hanka sits next to me as we perform our work using sewing machines.

There are windows on all four sides of the fur shop. From one of the windows near my work, I witness terrifying acts taking place on a little hill called *Cipowy Dotek*.

Until mid-February of 1944, killings were held on *Hujowa Gorka*. This larger hill was named after the surname of SS-*Unterscharführer* Albert Hujar who ordered the original executions. When the site could no longer be used for the killings, barracks were built on top of it. The execution site was moved to *Cipowy Dotek*. Some prisoners still refer to this hill as *Hujowa Gorka*. It's a horrific place, whatever name they call it.

Almost daily during morning count, the SS select prisoners in poor health who can't do the work. They march these prisoners to a large pit on this little hill. I see them ordered to undress and forced to line up at the edge of the pit. The SS uncover a machine gun. I hear the rapid popping sound of fire. The prisoners are shot and fall down into the pit. Wounded prisoners still alive are buried along with the other victims. They are all covered with a layer of ground lime. The pit is then ready for the next day's victims.

It's impossible to erase these images and sounds from my mind. Prisoners are looked upon as subhuman, to be killed at any given time.

Is the SS choosing to inflict more suffering upon us by having us witness these killings? Is it not enough that we already know how sadistic these bastards are? Plaszow is a living hell.

I try suppressing the horror of these killings as I press my foot to the sewing machine pedal. I need to keep my wits about me. I have to do everything I can to will myself to stay alive.

What astonishes me is that many of the victims murdered in Plaszow are prominent business and religious leaders. These are people who held important positions in Krakow before the war. Their status means nothing to these Nazi killers. We are nameless, bodies to be worked to the bones.

Other terrifying unthinkable killings take place on the hill at night. Plaszow is limited to a certain number of prisoners. I don't know how many. There's a standing order to exterminate the excess number of prisoners to make room for new arrivals. Jewish policemen are assigned to roundup prisoners who don't have valuable work assignments. These prisoners are put into a fenced-off square.

It's common knowledge that German guards come to the square at night. They walk the prisoners up the hill and then shoot them. Whenever a young prisoner is put into the fenced-off square, a few Jewish policemen take it upon themselves to exchange an old person with a young person.

Is it right for these Jewish policemen to play G-d? My youth gives me an edge. But what about someone like Hanka's father? He could be exchanged for a younger prisoner. It's a moral question that begs to be answered at another time, who shall live and who shall die.

Chapter 20

1944 – No One Is Safe

Jozek

Wilek Chilowicz is Hanka's uncle. He is the brother to her mother, Malia, and to her aunt, Frania. He is the Jewish Commandant and Chief Jewish Administrator of the Plaszow concentration camp.

Chilowicz wields enormous power over the prisoners. He works for Goeth and helps him amass wealth from Krakow's black market by dealing in illegal activities. Using his contacts in Krakow, he sells things for Goeth, such as confiscated jewelry from the transports of prisoners.

All of a sudden Hanka's uncle is a big shot. Chilowicz's wife, Marysia, is a policewoman. They wear custom uniforms tailored out of expensive light brown material and custom fake-leather black boots. They carry whips on themselves and don't hesitate to use them on prisoners. The couple's power has created terror and hatred among prisoners. Chilowicz is a tall handsome man, full head of dark brown hair, and has an athletic build. He's a son of a bitch.

To Chilowicz's credit, he has attempted to keep prisoners in Plaszow alive. On May 14, 1943, he came to the rescue of Roman, Wilus, and other children when the Germans ordered a mass roundup.

Youngsters, under the age of fourteen, were gathered up because they didn't contribute to the forced labor. The Germans played songs like "*Gute Nacht Mutte*r", Good Night Mother, over loudspeakers trying to mask the shock of taking the children away from their parents.

There were hundreds of SS men surrounding the *Appellplatz* with guns aiming towards the prisoners. Dogs barked. Germans beat hysterical parents clinging to their crying and screaming children. Children were forced onto waiting wagons. The violence was unbearable to witness. These innocent children did no harm.

They're Jewish. That's all the Germans care about in taking them away from their parents.

Hanka's brother, Manek, was given advance notice from Chilowicz. He knew the children were going to be transported to the Auschwitz extermination camp. Manek alerted Roman and Wilus to hide in the latrine, along with some other children. The Germans keep their distance from the twelve-foot deep latrine because it gives off a repulsive stench.

Chilowicz did what he could to save all the children from the roundup. Manek told Hanka their uncle argued with Goeth to allow all the children to stay in Plaszow. Goeth refused his pleas.

One August morning, I walk in a group with men from the barracks as I head to the fur shop. Hanka received her assignment through Chilowicz, and she is the one who got me the assignment. She begged her uncle to give it to me. As labor goes, it's a good one. A prisoner, also assigned to the fur shop, revealed to me Hanka told Chilowicz I was her husband. Smart girl.

Plaszow is built on two Jewish cemeteries and has several layers of barbed wires. The Germans operate and live primarily outside the perimeter of the fence within the Jewish camp. Further uphill the road divides and a narrow road leads up a hill to Goeth's villa, "Grey House".

To reach the fur shop, I must walk past a chain-link fence from the living quarters to the industrial part of Plaszow, the labor working camp. I also walk past Jewish guards. The factories are located next to the men's camp. The women's barracks are on the hill. They walk a little farther downhill to reach the working area.

Manek, Sabcia, and I try to seek each other out when we walk to our assignments. Most days, like today, I don't see them. I worry about my brother and sister. They need to keep their strength up physically and mentally to survive. They mustn't do anything that will get them in trouble or call attention to them.

Manek works in the Madritsch uniform factory. Sabcia is assigned to the printing shop. Hanka's cousin Rena Ferber, and Rena's mother, Rose, work there. Huge bales of paper for printing are brought in that come out ruled and lined.

The Madritsch factory, located about two hundred feet from the fur shop, operates round the clock. Prisoners working in the factory sew new uniforms for the German army. The factory complex has a few separate barracks not enclosed by any fence from the other working areas.

Hanka's uncle, Henryk, is a member of the Jewish police force and a camp superintendent in charge of Madritsch. His wife, Frania, works with him at the Madritsch factory. Frania's brother, Chilowicz, was instrumental in Henryk becoming a Jewish policeman and getting both of them their assignments to Madritsch.

As the men from the barracks and I turn the corner walking to our assignments, something catches my eye. I see Marysia Chilowicz standing behind the corner of the first barracks. She's visible only to someone who turns his head in her direction. She's a petite woman, about five-feet-tall with blond hair.

She looks different. Marysia is dressed in civilian clothes. She is not wearing her usual Jewish policewoman uniform. I don't acknowledge her and continue walking toward the fur shop.

Somewhere in my mind it clicks. *Why isn't Marysia wearing her brown police uniform and shiny black boots?* I enter the shop shortly before Hanka.

Later in the morning, Hanka and I are sitting next to each other at our sewing machines when a prisoner calls softly to us from the open window. "Hanka. Jozek. Chilowiczes are murdered."

"What?" Stunned, I leap up from my chair and rush over to the window. He's gone.

"Oh. No. Can't be!" Hanka cries out.

I search the grounds for any movement. I look in the direction of the little hill where people are murdered. Nothing. I rush to the other windows in the shop. There's no unusual activity outside.

I come back to Hanka and take hold of her hands. "Stop crying. Get a hold of yourself. We must act normal."

"Why kill them?" Hanka asks, her body shaking. "I don't understand."

"You know they don't need reasons to murder."

"What about Manek? He works for Uncle Wilek. Oh, G-d. What if something happens to my brother?"

"Don't jump to conclusions. He should be okay."

But is he? I don't know what the hell is going on. My hands are sticky with sweat. I feel the heat circling my neck. Are they coming after Hanka and her family? What about me? Am I in danger?

I try to logically ponder our situation. Should we stay in place? Here we're trapped, no place to hide. Should we go outside?

We'll be exposed. Should we go to the barracks? We'll be separated. There are no satisfying answers. I don't know what to do.

Hanka's quiet sobbing is muffled by the sounds of sewing machines handled by nearly one hundred prisoners assigned to the fur shop. German guards can walk in at any time and count how many fur products we have completed. We repair German soldiers' heavy lamb fur coats torn from their fighting at the Russian front.

Along with the coats, German guards and soldiers come to the shop for fur slippers. Since it has become known we can sew slippers, the guards order them for their wives and girlfriends.

"Uncle Wilek works for Goeth. My uncle is an important man, head of the Jewish police," Hanka says.

Then it hits me. "I saw your aunt this morning. I thought something was not right. She was hiding behind the barracks dressed in civilian clothes."

"Civilian clothes? That's strange."

Suddenly, a prisoner at the door frantically calls out to us, "Henryk and Frania are dead. Shot." He pushes little Wilus inside the shop.

I jump out of my chair and run on the pieces of lumber and half-packed dirt floor to the door. Wilus rushes past me to Hanka. The prisoner is gone. Panic rises through my body. Pressure knocks against my chest. My throat closes up.

"Mamusia, Tatus, shot." Wilus buries himself into Hanka's arms and gushes tears.

"Where? When?" I ask.

"He said, he said, Mamusia and Tatus were killed."

"Shush. You're okay. You're with us," Hanka says holding him snug against her body.

"Who killed them? Who took you here? What did he tell you?" I pepper him rapidly with questions.

"The man said, the prisoner said Goeth killed Mamusia and Tatus."

"Goeth? Are you sure it was him, the commandant?"

"I was playing. I wasn't there. That's what he told me."

"What happened after the prisoner said they were killed?"

"He grabbed my hand and told me to run fast with him to the fur shop, to Hanka and you."

Why would Goeth himself kill his parents? It makes no sense. Will the Germans come looking for Wilus? I need to hide him. I take Wilus out of Hanka's arms and look into his red watery eyes. "Listen to me. We must keep you hidden. Stop crying."

Exhaustion overtakes him. His legs begin to buckle. "I want you to lie down under the table. We'll put the guards' coats and furs on top of you. Hanka and I will be working next to you. Don't worry. You will be safe with us."

He lies down on the floor as I tell him. He places his hands under his face and bends his legs on top of pieces of fur on the floor between our sewing tables. Hanka and I pile the heavy coats and mounds of fur pieces on top of him leaving air openings for him to breathe.

A prisoner working at the sewing machine nearby breaks his silence. "Why kill his parents and the Chilowiczes?"

"I don't know. I can't process it now. We have to act normal, like nothing out of the ordinary happened."

Hanka whispers to me, "Manek worked for our uncle. Aunt Frania and Uncle Henryk worked at Madritsch. Mamusia and Tatus, oh my G-d, are they safe?"

"Your brother, Manek, is smart and probably hiding. Your parents have no dealings with Goeth." I try to allay her fears while mine continue to spiral.

"I don't understand why they were all shot. Uncle Wilek is in a position of power. Why would Goeth murder Aunt Frania and Uncle Henryk?"

"Hanka, *proszę*, please, take control of yourself. We need to keep pace with our workload. We can't let our guard down."

I gently wipe warm tears off of her face with a small piece of fur. Our eyes lock with fear before I place her hands on the sewing machine. "*Proszę*, Hanka, concentrate on the work. For now that's all we can do."

Why kill members of her family? I search my mind for an explanation of why these murders could have occurred. I can't think of any reason. None. Hanka and I are petrified someone will give us more news from the window about her family, or that a German soldier will come inside the fur shop looking for us.

Try as I might, I can't conjure an alternative to staying put and doing nothing. Somehow Hanka and I summon inner strength to keep up with our labor. Wilus continues to stay hidden on the floor. We learn nothing more about the murders.

In the evening when it's time to leave for the barracks, I move the coats and fur pieces off of Wilus' soaked sweaty body. I grab his hands to lift him up and wait a few seconds for his eyes to adjust to the light. So far we are safe, but I'm very nervous to go outside. Will Germans be waiting for us with guns drawn?

I do a cautious survey of the outside area from the shop's windows. I heave a sigh of relief when I don't see any Germans. Hoping we're not in immediate danger, I lead the way for the three of us to walk outside. I'm on my guard. We move toward the barracks, intermingling with the men and women prisoners coming from their assignments.

My mind twists around what we know and don't know. Wilus' parents were murdered by Goeth. Also killed were Hanka's aunt and uncle, Wilek and Marysia Chilowicz. The big question is why were they killed?

Before Hanka separates from us to go to the women's quarters, she kisses Wilus on his cheeks. She hugs him and tells him he'll be safe with me. Fresh tears drip down his face. Hanka brushes them away with her hand.

"Be brave Wilus. Don't worry. Jozek and I will take care of you." His small body quivers with fear. Hanka squeezes his hand. "You are safe with us. I promise."

I take his small hand from hers into mine and tell him we have to go. We are in the way of prisoners passing us on their way to their barracks. I don't need anyone stopping and asking questions about him. It's never good to be noticed. Hanka and I give a swift nod goodbye, and she heads to the women's barracks.

Wilus and I walk through the fence to the men's barracks. From now on he is ours – Hanka's and mine. No more are there a mother and father for this eight-year-old boy.

That late summer evening, Germans order the entire camp to march out of their barracks to the *Appellplatz*. Before I go out, I hide Wilus under a bottom shelf and warn him not to make a sound, not to move from his place. I'm worried about looking after him, but I'm also worried about my own life. Germans could be searching for Wilus right now. He's not out of danger. I could be punished, even killed, for hiding him.

At the *Appellplatz*, Jewish prisoners have laid out dead bodies in a line. We're forced to look at the corpses lying on the ground in their bloodied clothing with mouths open and flies buzzing around. It takes all of my willpower to push down and swallow the bile rising in my throat.

No! Hanka's brother, Manek, is one of the dead. How will Hanka react? She mustn't cry out when she sees his body. Manek's corpse is lined up on the ground with her aunts and uncles: Wilek and Marysia Chilowicz, Frania and Henryk Schnitzer. Also killed was a male prisoner, no relation to the families.

I want to scream out to the Nazis, "You are the filth of the earth! How can you look at yourselves in the face?" What I want to do and what I do are two different things. I am silent.

I read the place cards tied to the corpses' chests, "Those Who Violate Just Laws Can Expect A Similar Death."

What laws did they violate? Doesn't add up. I keep my burning anger under control and hide my emotions as I follow my barracks' line. I can't let these stinking Nazis get the better of me. What the hell did these members of Hanka's family do to deserve this? After all of us prisoners view the corpses, there are designated prisoners who will put the bodies into a mass grave.

I am puzzled by their killings. The unknown unnerves me, always has. I try to figure out what happened.

I've always been a logical person. I observe now that the Chilowiczes are the only ones dressed differently. They're wearing civilian clothes. Wilus' parents are dressed in their normal camp clothing. His father has an insignia of factory supervisor on his shoulder epaulet.

A German officer shouts threats to us before we leave the *Appellplatz*, "This is what happens to prisoners who try to escape!"

Escape? This is the first we hear they tried to escape. Why would they want to escape? The Chilowiczes had power in Plaszow. Wilus' parents wouldn't go without him. Hanka's brother wouldn't leave without telling his family. Lies. All lies. The Germans are spouting lies.

They don't care that we witness this brutality. The Germans expect us to die from starvation or slave labor, if they don't kill us first. I try to ignore the shivers of fear shooting down my body on this August evening. I promise myself I will survive. I will meet the ongoing challenge of staying alive. I will live to bear witness to these grisly crimes.

We discover why Hanka's family members were murdered. We learn from Jewish policemen that Goeth is going to be transferred, and the Plaszow labor camp is to be shut down. The Jewish policemen say Goeth was afraid his black market activities would be exposed.

The story goes that Goeth was terrified Wilek and Marysia Chilowicz would be sent to a camp where they would barter their knowledge about his illegal dealings. Goeth made a false report to Wilhelm Koppe, the SS police chief of the Government General. Goeth said there was a potential camp revolt going to take place by Wilek Chilowicz and other Jewish prisoners. He sought authorization to murder Chilowicz and the others on these false charges. Goeth got the consent he wanted.

Manek, Hanka's brother, was Chilowicz's secretary. He spoke German and did writing for the camp. Through Chilowicz he knew about Goeth's shady deals on the black market. Manek had gone to Goeth's villa on business. That's why he was killed.

A prisoner told us Manek was on a hill when a voice over the microphone summoned him to go see Goeth. This was a normal occurrence. Manek told another prisoner, as he ran down the hill, to tell his mother he loved her. He must have had a premonition something was going to happen.

A German officer grabbed him by his left arm at the bottom of the hill. With his right hand Manek reached for the officer's pistol and hit him in the face. The gun fell to the ground. The officer picked up the pistol and shot Manek twice.

Margot Schlesinger is assigned to the Madritsch factory in the shipping department warehouse. Her job is to see how many ready-made items, such as uniforms are in one bag before the bags are thrown out from the factory's front window on the first floor. Non-Jewish Polish truck drivers load them onto trucks.

She was Frania's friend and an eyewitness to Wilus' parents being shot. She told Hanka and I how they were murdered.

Margot recalled Wilek Chilowicz was enraged the day before the murders. He had come to the shipping department. He wanted to get something from the back of the materials warehouse, and she went with him. She overheard him saying, "We're not going to let them get away with this. We're going to fight!" She had no idea what he was talking about. She did not look at him, kept quiet, and saw him leave.

At work the next day, Margot went with Frania to the latrine. Frania told her Goeth had a search made of her brother's quarters. A pistol was discovered. Frania said her brother didn't remember Goeth ever having given it to him. She said it had to have been planted there.

Later that same day, Frania's husband, Henryk, started to walk into the officers' barracks when Goeth called out to him, "Where's your wife?"

Henryk called to Frania to come out of the barracks. Goeth took out his pistol, shot Henryk first and then Frania in the back.

We learned Wilek Chilowicz had heard of Goeth's being transferred and doubted he would be able to leave Plaszow alive. An SS auxiliary officer pretended to offer him an escape deal. Chilowicz was told he could get the whole family out of the camp in one of the large fuel-burning trucks. Chilowicz was willing to pay in diamonds for the transportation.

Wilek and Marysia Chilowicz hid in the material shed and then were taken to hide in the truck. They were driven to the gate where the wagon was stopped. An illegal gun was found tucked inside Wilek Chilowicz's boot. His pockets had diamonds. Goeth's story was that he saved Plaszow from an insurgency by executing the plot's leaders.

The other prisoner killed was Mr. Finklestein. I don't know why. He had no connection to Hanka's family.

There are rumblings throughout the camp about the deaths. Prisoners fear that if Wilek Chilowicz, who was close to Goeth, could be shot, then no one is safe. Who will be murdered next?

Life is hell. No time for mourning.

Chapter 21

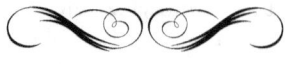

Staying Alive

Wilus

I hide in Mr. Jacob Heubenstock's quarters in the barracks during the day and stay until lights go out at night. Jozek knows Mr. Heubenstock from his Krakow sports club. Jozek tells me I'm lucky he allows me to stay in his quarters. He says Mr. Heubenstock is risking his life for me. If the Germans find me there, he will probably get killed. Jozek goes on and on about how lucky I am.

I'm not a baby. I know things. Mr. Heubenstock is a nice man. He got the barracks' supervisor job through Uncle Wilek. Because Mr. Heubenstock is a supervisor, he has a room to himself in the barracks. Early in the morning when prisoners leave the barracks, I come to his quarters.

Mr. Heubenstock warns me not to make any noise so the Germans will not find out I'm in his room. The Germans check the barracks for people who have no work assignments. Unless the Germans have a reason to suspect something, they won't search his place. I thank him for hiding me. I tell him he doesn't have to worry. I promise I won't do anything to get him in trouble.

There's nothing to do all day but stay on Mr. Heubenstock's cot or walk quietly around his room. It's easy to tell if the Germans come to the barracks. Their boots make noise.

I think about Mamusia and Tatus all the time. I wish someone would kill Goeth like he killed Mamusia and Tatus. Roman told me Goeth rides on a white horse with a gun in his hand. He shoots prisoners for no reason.

Jozek said all the prisoners in Plaszow were forced to walk next to the dead bodies lying on the ground. Mamusia, Tatus, Aunt Marysia, Uncle Wilek, and Manek were murdered. I don't want to believe it happened, but Jozek said it's true.

Sometimes when Manek warned Roman and me about *Aktions*, we would hide in Aunt Marysia's and Uncle Wilek's quarters. They lived in a small wooden building that stood alone, not in any barracks. The building had a living room and kitchen combination, a bedroom, and a bathroom. I wasn't afraid of Germans coming into their quarters. It felt safe there. It was good to be with Roman and not have to hide by myself.

Now I'm staying alive, but I'm alone. There's no Roman to play with. I want Mamusia and Tatus to be with me. I want Mamusia to hug me. I want Tatus to take care of me.

I miss my cousin Manek. He would take Roman, me, and other children to the magazine shop to play. The shop has blankets and clothing taken from prisoners forced to come to Plaszow. I have a friend, Naftali, who plays in the magazine shop too. He is about my age. His hair is white, and he wears glasses. Whenever we heard the Germans come into the shop, everyone ran and hid behind the storage shelves. The Germans didn't stay long in the magazine shop. They never found us.

A few months ago in May, Germans rounded up children and took them from their parents. Music played over loudspeakers while Germans forced the children to be loaded into trucks. I was scared. I didn't know what was happening. I was in the magazine shop. Roman came for me. We ran fast to hide in the wooden building and down into the latrine.

At the latrine you step onto large boards. The smell is sickening. It comes up my nose, into my mouth, and burns my eyes. There were shouts and people running on the outside. Roman told me to stop crying, but he didn't stuff my cap in my mouth or call me crybaby. I don't like when he does that. I'm not a baby.

The latrine has trenches dug in the ground. Telephone poles lay down at the edge. You sit on the boards to do what you have to do. Shit falls down. There are crossbars under the poles. This is where we took cover, between the crossbars in the holes above the shit. We had to hold on tight so we would not drown. It's mostly dark. Only a little light comes from above the holes where you sit when you do your business. Flies buzz around. It's safe to hide here because the stink keeps the German guards away.

Roman and I hid with other kids in the latrine for two days without any food. We talked in whispers and joked about the stinking smell. We knew the *Aktion* was over when prisoners started to come to the latrine. The Germans' boots make different sounds on the boards.

A few women prisoners called for us to come out. They took us to the *Krankenstube*, the prisoners' sickroom. Germans don't like to come to the sickroom because they're afraid of getting sick.

Before Tatus was killed, he sewed clothing for Roman and me: beige knickers, a shirt, a long sleeve jacket, and a round hat with blue and white stripes. We changed from those clothes after we came out of hiding in the latrine. It was hard to get the stinky smell out of our wooden shoes.

Only a few of us kids are left in Plaszow. We're the lucky ones. We escaped the roundup. The big difference for me is the other kids have their parents alive.

There is no one to talk to or play with all day. I have to keep myself invisible. I think about when I was little and lived in Krakow with Mamusia and Tatus. I sat on Tatus' lap. He read me bedtime stories. Mamusia took me to the park to play. We ate dinner together in the kitchen. Before I went to sleep, I had milk and cake. My stomach makes noises. I'm always hungry.

When Mr. Heubenstock comes back to his quarters, he hands me a metal cup with some soup and a piece of bread to eat. I thank him very much for the food. Aunt Malia works in the camp kitchen and gives him food for me. It's not enough to stop my stomach from hurting. Mr. Heubenstock lets me know when I can go back to the barracks.

I hide behind Jozek in the corner on the third shelf. There's a ladder leaning against the shelves to climb to the top. Jozek says it's better to be on the top shelf, that the corner gives us more room. I'm squeezed against him on the hard wooden shelf, sleeping head–to-toe. I try to make room between us, but I can't. Our bodies touch. I feel the hardness of the wood under my head. A few pieces of straw were once on the shelf, but they are gone now.

I hear noises in the barracks at night. Prisoners cry, some scream out. Others pray to G-d. Jozek hardly says anything to me before he falls asleep. The prisoners' smells from their sweaty bodies on the shelves mixes in with the hot air. It stinks. I close my eyes, but I can't sleep. I miss Mamusia and Tatus.

Mamusia held my hand when we walked with Tatus to the factory. I liked the touch of her hand. Tatus told me I needed to obey him and stay out of everyone's way when they got to their work assignments.

If I didn't go to the magazine shop, I was allowed to stay in the factory. Mamusia hugged me before she started her work in the materials warehouse. Her friend Mrs. Schlesinger worked in the shipping department. I liked her. She always smiled at me.

Everyone was scared of the Germans. I sat on the floor in the factory against the wall. I thought about having an army of Polish Jews. The army would get all the prisoners out of Plaszow and shoot the Germans, bang, bang, bang!

I don't like to think about the day when Mamusia and Tatus were killed. I was in the magazine shop when a prisoner called out for me. He talked fast and said we had to run to Hanka and her boyfriend, Jozek, in the fur shop. The prisoner said Goeth killed my parents. I didn't have time to think. I didn't want to believe him. He took my hand, and we ran out of the shop.

I was out of breath when the prisoner pushed me into the fur shop. He called out to Hanka and Jozek from the doorway and told them Mamusia and Tatus were killed. He ran away before they could ask him questions.

Jozek asked me what happened. I couldn't answer him. I didn't know what was true or not true. I wasn't with Mamusia and Tatus. The prisoner could be wrong. Everything happened in a rush when the prisoner came to the magazine shop to get me.

I couldn't stop crying when Jozek asked me questions. It's good Roman wasn't there to call me a crybaby. Jozek hid me on the floor between the tables. He piled furs and coats on top of me. My shirt rolled up and stuck to my body. My eyes burned. I heard Jozek and Hanka talking about Hanka's brother, Manek. My stomach growled. I was hungry and thirsty. I fell asleep.

I woke up when Jozek took the furs and coats off of me. The hot air felt good on my face. My body was sweaty. Hanka and Jozek told me they would take care of me, that I would be okay. I'm not okay.

We walked from the fur shop to the living quarters with the other prisoners. I didn't know what to think about Mamusia and Tatus killed by Goeth. Hanka held onto my hand. She hugged and kissed me before she left for the women's barracks. She told me not to worry. How can I not worry?

This is the worst thing for me. I don't have Mamusia and Tatus. I sleep next to Jozek, but I am alone.

Chapter 22

Plaszow 1944 -I Pick a Trade

Jozek

"Come quick, you have an assignment," a Jewish foreman orders me. I match his hurried pace to the center square.

I meet up with other men who, like me, have been taken off of their normal labor assignments. We are commanded to stand in line and take a shovel off of a truck. Then we have the gruesome task of digging up bodies from mass graves and burning them.

The Germans responding to the Russian army approaching from the east are on the offensive. The Germans are on a mission to erase any evidence of their atrocities. They want to hide the truth.

Before burning the bodies, three men are designated to salvage for valuables, such as wedding bands and any diamonds dead prisoners could have had drilled into their molars. Prisoners put teeth and gold or diamonds into a wooden box about fifteen-inches long and one-foot wide held on the lap of a German soldier. A prisoner, who is a dentist, has the gruesome assignment to drill the gold and diamonds out of the teeth.

The fresh smell of September air is destroyed by the pungent scent of dead bodies. My eyes are red. I gag on the stench. I do this work for two days. The odor of these nameless bodies sucks up the oxygen. It could be me lying there. My salvation in all this is in knowing the Nazis fear the advancing Red army. Their day will come.

The fire burns for weeks. The sky is contaminated with black smoke. There is no escaping the gray ashes absorbed into my body. The smell lingers on my skin. I taste it in my mouth. It clings to my nostrils. Life is unbearable. Somehow I make it through.

Hanka and I are terrified by the horrendous unpredictable actions of Goeth and what he will do next. We're afraid the Germans could find Wilus. We think he is relatively safe hidden in Jacob's quarters during the day and with me at the barracks at night. But what if the Germans make a surprise search. Wilus is disposable to Goeth. He's a kid. He has no value to the Germans.

Hanka and I convince ourselves we are somewhat less worried Goeth will kill her parents. If he wanted them killed, they would be dead already. Roman is safe for the time being. His father said he was older than he is and got him a job in the paper and printing factory working next to him.

Wilus does what I tell him to do. Hiding to him is normal. He's quiet and keeps to himself. I don't know what he thinks. I have no experience with kids.

Rumors circulate that with the liquidation of Plaszow, prisoners will be shipped to various camps. It's said a list is being compiled of people who will be sent to Oscar Schindler's factory, a new plant near his hometown in Brunnlitz, Czechoslovakia. The factory will produce ammunition for the German army.

Schindler is an ethnic German and a Catholic. His factory, which was originally owned by a Jew, was relocated from his defunct enamelware plant in Zablocie, outside of Krakow. In the Zablocie plant, Schindler's laborers turned out pots, pans, and mess kits for the German military.

Schindler has arranged for the transfer of about eight hundred Jewish men and three hundred Jewish women from Plaszow to work at his new ammunition factory. To get on Schindler's List, you must be a very important person, have a needed skill, or bribe a Jewish *kapo*, policeman, with gold or money. Prisoners from Krakow who worked for Schindler have some priority in being put on this list.

As you can imagine, everyone is desperate to get on the list. Schindler's List is a lifeline, a chance for survival. Reports say no one gets killed at the factory, and Schindler treats workers as human beings. Schindler is like a miracle, a shining force in our desperate lives.

I have nothing to bribe the *kapos* with, but that doesn't stop me. Forcing all my energy into getting my name on the list, I frantically contact any person I know from before the war. I especially concentrate on people from my sports activities. I am relentless in seeking out anyone who can possibly have any influence.

Unless you are a tradesman, you wind up digging ditches, so I pick a trade, *elektriker*, electrician. Good fortune is with me. My name is put on the list.

I stay on top of the situation by encouraging my contacts to see to it that my name is kept on the list. Bribery is ongoing. Names are easily removed to make room for others. Each day I am on the list I am closer to survival. I can't let up asking people to make sure my name is kept on Schindler's List.

Hanka and her parents, Leon and Malia, her brother, Roman, and her cousin, Wilus, are also on Schindler's List. Hanka's brother, Manek, must have put their names on the list before he was killed. I have no way of knowing, but maybe Manek was responsible for getting me on the list too.

But tragedy slaps me down again. I can't do anything to get my sister and brother, Sabcia and Manek, on the list. It's unknown what camp they will be forced to go to from Plaszow. Extermination camps cannot be ruled out. We're aware of these camps but don't know how prisoners are killed. Panic pains circulate throughout my body. My heart palpitates. My throat closes up. What will happen to them? Where is Mamusia?

Her face polished with wet tears, Sabcia grabs my hand. "Jozek, you have the best chance of survival. You must live for our family."

"You and Manek will survive." I look over my shoulder to Manek. "We will be together when this is over, with Mamusia too."

"Yes," Manek says. His voice cracks. "We will survive. None of us will be beaten down."

"You must be strong, preserve your strength, and keep up your spirits. The coming of the Russians is a good sign. You'll see. It will all work out to our advantage."

Damn. Damn. Why couldn't I get them on Schindler's List? We are going to be separated, and I can't do anything about it.

Chapter 23

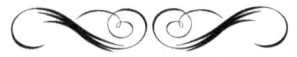

Like Spoons in a Drawer

Jozek

Five a.m., Sunday, October 15, 1944, I wait anxiously with Leon, Roman, and Wilus to be transported to Schindler's factory in Brunnlitz, Czechoslovakia. Hanka and her mother will leave a week later with the other women on Schindler's List.

Yesterday I cut out photos of Hanka and me from our Plaszow identity cards. I gave her mine and kept hers. I told Hanka I loved her and would always carry her photo with me. She pressed my card against her heart and said she loved me too. She is animated about going to Schindler's factory, saying how our lives will be saved. She tried to console me by telling me that my family would survive.

I want to believe they will survive. Not knowing where Sabcia and Manek will be transported to from Plaszow doesn't give me any reassurance. I worry about Mamusia. Where is she? I'm head of our family and helpless. All I can do is hope they will be strong, vigilant, and outlive the murderous Germans.

The *Schindlerjuden*, Schindler's Jews, are assembled on the *Appellplatz*. Guards shove us onto boxcars coupled to cars containing thirteen hundred prisoners. I lean against a side of the boxcar sandwiched in between two men. Body odors intermingle with the stifled air. I am fortunate to be on the list. My contacts or Hanka's brother, Manek's, came through for me.

Damn. Why couldn't I get my sister and brother on the list? I can't stop thinking about them. I analyze what more I could have done. If only I had money or diamonds for a bribe.

We were given three hundred grams of bread that has to last for the trip to the factory. I mustn't eat it all at once.

It's good Malia and Hanka will be transported to the factory together. Hanka will look out for her mother. People say Schindler is a good man. He's friendly with the SS, the Nazi elite. He has a reputation of being a risk-taker. People say we will be safe at his factory. I have to believe we will get through this.

Leon is edging Roman and Wilus to the corner of the boxcar. Leon is a good man. He tries his best to be positive. Roman told me he wishes he could believe his father when he says everything will be all right for us. Roman says he learns what people think by overhearing their conversations and taking in what's happening. He's a smart kid.

Roman says, as I move closer to him, Leon, and Wilus, "The stink from the shit burns my throat, clings to my clothes, and sticks to me like a bee to skin."

Wilus is looking down at the boxcar floor. I wonder what he's thinking. Roman is pressing him against the wall. Everyone is squeezed in tight.

"I'm cold," Wilus says when he raises his head. "The stink burns my nose."

"It's temporary. You'll see, things will be better when we get to Schindler's factory," I tell him.

I try ignoring my endless stomach growls. We have been on the freight train for three days when it slows and then stops. Boxcar doors are unlocked. The SS shout and run among us jabbing with their rifles at our bodies. They yell for us to take off our clothes for disinfection.

I throw my clothing into one of the piles and walk in what seems to be a nice little town. Germans stare at our naked bodies. The cold air shocks my insides and releases some of the pungent smell of vomit and piss that engulfed me in the freight train. It takes about 4 kilometers, about 2½ miles, to reach the subcamp of Schindler's factory, Gross-Rosen, Big Roses.

A German guard calls out prisoners' names from a list. When the guard asks Wilus for his birthdate, he looks down and stares at the ground. He has no clue as to what he should answer. I'm standing next to him and am prepared for this. I whisper a date. He repeats it to the guard.

Hanka and I had discussed his birthdate. She asked her parents. They told us they aren't sure of the exact month but said it's close to Roman's birthday in January. They picked a day in April and a year. Damn those Germans with their lists.

By six in the evening, we are lined up on the ice-covered *Appellplatz*. Snow covers the ground in the woods. The SS wearing overcoats walk among our naked bodies and lash out at prisoners who cannot stop shivering. I will my body to be still. I think back to before the German invasion, a hot summer Krakow day. *I jump into the water. I am the daredevil of my friends.* I am not brave now with my body frozen, my stomach empty, my teeth chattering.

All night from early evening, we are forced to stand on the *Appellplatz* because there are no huts available to house us. I'll get through this. The important thing is I am one of Schindler's Jews. We stand through the night to midmorning of the next day until the SS herd us into the showers.

Wilus is lucky. A prisoner gave him a glass of milk before we went to the showers. He gulped the milk down. I would have done the same. We are all hungry and thirsty.

What's the matter with this kid? I put a five-dollar gold-coin, one of two that I have, in the crease of Wilus' behind after we were examined. I thought he would have enough sense to hold it in tight when he was in the shower. I let him know I was upset with him, more than upset, angry.

Before we were marched to the showers, I managed to tape the other coin with flesh-colored medical tape to the bottom of my right foot. It was undetected. I found the two gold-coins hidden in Mamusia's bedroom closet before we were forced to leave for the ghetto. I've kept them with me ever since. I figured I might need them to bribe someone. My father must have gotten the coins on the black market. I know he didn't trust Polish currency.

Can't do anything about the gold-coin now. What's with Wilus not concentrating and squeezing his behind tight? I didn't ask him to do anything difficult.

After the cold shower, a barber shaved our heads and body parts. I'm dressed in a striped prison uniform and shoes that are too small. I stretch my head up and barely see Leon, Roman, and Wilus on the hallway floor ahead of me.

Wilus is stacked in front of Roman, who is stacked in front of Leon. German guards have crammed the Schindler prisoners into three huts on the cold concrete floor with no blankets. We are squeezed together sitting with one man backed up between the legs of the man behind his own open legs, who gives support to the man in front. We're frozen in position. We're packed in tight, front to back, like spoons in a drawer.

Guards sit on chairs against the wall armed with truncheons. When a prisoner needs to use the latrine, he has to walk over the prisoners' heads and shoulders.

During the days we spend in this transit camp, Gross-Rosen, I experience barbarity not known to me until now. The camp is located at a mountain by a stone quarry in Lower Silesia. Murderers run this camp.

It's the first camp created by Hitler for homosexuals and criminals. Homosexuals are forced to wear a pink sign on their pocket. Political murderers wear a red sign. Criminals wear a green triangle. Schindler prisoners wear a Star of David consisting of two triangles, one yellow and one red. The yellow triangle represents a Jew, the red triangle a political prisoner.

It's madness. Prisoners are forced to carry heavy pieces of granite up the steep sides of the quarry where they can easily slip and fall to their death. I witness forty to fifty dead prisoners being brought down from the mountain on stretchers to the plaza just to be counted. My eyes register this evil taking place, engraving the horror in my mind.

Since we are in transit to Schindler's factory and have no work assignment here, guards assemble us in front of barracks after the morning count. No matter what the weather, we're forced to stand in line for about ten hours. The SS shoot prisoners who fall down.

My thoughts wander all over the place. *I took the risk of getting past the supervisor's door without his seeing me and smuggling the extra set of linens into the ghetto. Lucky I did not get caught cutting pieces of the maroon velvet off of the backs of the train seats. I wonder how the Russian commandant knew me. He saved me. Lucky again, when the Russian officer took my bribe for selling sausages on the black market.* Boom! I straighten my body at the sound of a gun blast. Another prisoner is shot.

I catch sight of Wilus in line when the gunshot goes off. He straightens his stance, keeps his hands stiff at his sides, and tries to control shaking his body. Nothing I can do to eliminate his panic. I'm full of nerves myself. No one knows who will be shot next.

Schindler prisoners are given artificial coffee, a dark brown fluid, for our morning meal. My stomach aches for more food. We get a break from standing in line in front of the barracks for lunch. Lunch consists of very little soup that tastes like dirty water.

If you're fortunate, the Jewish prisoner who doles out the soup will give you some kind of solid, less than a sliver of a potato, in the watery liquid. Our meal at night is a slice of bread. Rumors circulate that some prisoners are killed in order that Germans gain extra slices of bread at the evening distribution. I think there is a certain truth to this. I put nothing past the Germans.

In the evenings after the watery soup, prisoners are permitted to walk around the hut to converse with each other. This is our chance to talk. Leon and I keep up our morale by telling each other and the boys we are Schindler's men and will be getting out of this death camp. It can't be soon enough.

Nine p.m. comes and a whistle blasts. Guards shout for us to move fast. It's time for us to be counted and take our spoon positions on the floor for the night.

On our third day at Gross-Rosen, we are taken to the delousing stations for another shower. We are leaving. Guards march us out to boxcars with one slice of bread for food. Not knowing how long the trip to Schindler's factory will be, I caution myself to eat small bites of the bread. I take bites at intervals to try to quiet my stomach pains.

We squat on floorboards with no room to sit or lay down. As the cattle cars move, our bodies jerk. We are forced to bump into each other. I look up at one of two peephole windows with icicles attached. The absence of air moving around inside is suffocating. I finish eating my slice of bread on the first day. The trip takes about two days to reach the Zwittau depot. Thank G-d we left that hellhole Gross-Rosen behind.

We march through town in early morning darkness. Under the guard of German soldiers, we proceed almost 6½ kilometers, 4 miles, out into the hills following a rail siding. We enter the grounds, past metal gates with its electric fence to the factory.

Our quarters are in a two-story industrial barracks built around a courtyard. There are separate barracks for women. The ground floor has a high ceiling. I'm dressed in a blue and white striped uniform with numbers on my pocket matching my number on Schindler's List. This number 69187 will keep me alive.

Before I plop onto straw to sleep on the floor, I look around for Leon and the boys. Good, I see them sleeping across the room. Steam heat from boilers warms my body, my eyes close. This feels good.

Oscar Schindler is a handsome slender man, about six-feet-four-inches. He has broad shoulders, thick blond hair, and deep blue eyes. Schindler has us clean out the factory first. Then he has machinery delivered with which to make armaments. Guards check the list for prisoners with specific skills to perform their tasks. The SS guards are forbidden to enter the factory. Several Czech civilians are free to come and go from the camp. These civilians are the experienced people with skills to work the machinery.

As an *elektriker*, electrician, I am required to work outside during the most inclement weather. My numb fingers string electrical wire between the poles around the camp to form a fence. A civilian German, who is not in uniform and looks to me to be about eighty-years-old, is in charge. He can barely walk. He shuffles.

"You are no *elektriker*!" The German in charge shouts and waves his hand at me.

"I am an *elektriker*." I pull the wire tighter around the pole. "See."

"No *elektriker*," he repeats. "I report you to Schindler."

Sleep evades me at night. I'm frantic about what will happen to me. Will I get another assignment? Schindler won't send me to another camp. He mustn't.

The next day arrives with me reporting back to work. I focus on stringing the electrical wire. No one comes for me. The German in charge doesn't say anything to me. My luck holds out.

Hanka, her mother, and the other women on Schindler's List have not come from Plaszow. I learn they were sent to Auschwitz-Birkenau. We hear Schindler is trying to get them released to come to the factory. It can't be soon enough.

Chapter 24

1944, Early 1945 – Everything Happens Fast

Jozek

It happens in November when Schindler is away from the factory. It's a few weeks since we've been here. An inspector from Gross-Rosen comes with orders to search for children and to remove them from the factory. Their rational for doing this is that children do nothing to contribute to the manufacturing of arms.

Wilus and Roman are found playing among the abandoned spinning machines. A German guard commands them to come with him. About six or seven children are in the factory. The inspector's orders specify fathers must leave with their children. Their destination is Auschwitz-Birkenau.

We know about the Auschwitz-Birkenau extermination camp. Prisoners are gassed to death there. Damn! Damn! Nothing I can do. Schindler is away. If he were here, he would do something to prevent the children and their fathers from being forced to leave.

Everything happens fast. Kids are rounded up and escorted to the factory gate. Their fathers are ordered to go with them. As Leon rushes to the gate, he calls out to me that I should stay. He'll take Wilus with him. It makes sense. To stay here is survival. I can't give this up. Besides, I'm not Wilus' father.

Hanka will agree with me that this is the smart thing to do. Wilus will be okay going with her father. Leon can watch over both boys. Roman is a resourceful child.

I run to the gate to say goodbye to Leon, Wilus, and Roman. The boys sit on the ground with the other children. I won't leave Schindler's factory. I can't give this up.

As if this turn of events is not enough, I'm hit with more anguish and heartache. The women on Schindler's List finally arrive at the camp. Hanka's cousin, Rena, and Rena's mother are on the list. Hanka and her mother were left behind at Auschwitz-Birkeanu with the other women transported from Plaszow. Their names must have been removed from the list with bribes. What will happen to them? Will this captivity ever end? I'm heartbroken.

Later in the month, Viktor Lewis, a prisoner I played cards with in the Porgodze ghetto approaches me. He labors as an *elektriker* in my group to erect the fence around the factory. Viktor asks me to join the Brunnlitz underground. I vaguely know the camp has some kind of an underground.

Viktor explains that the underground's purpose is to help prisoners. Their aim is to have the Czechoslovakian underground come to our aid. Here's an opportunity to do something for us, to be elevated from our animal existence, to contribute to our survival. It's a chance to fight back. I say, "Yes," without any reservation.

The underground consists of thirty prisoners divided into two groups, three units in each group having a total of five men. Men are chosen based on their mental toughness. I vow not to give up any others in the resistance if I'm caught.

Our leader asked Schindler to contact the Czech underground leader to find out what help they could give to our covert operation. It's arranged that the Czech resistance will tell us what we should do before an *Aktion* takes place by the Germans.

We need to keep the Germans in place long enough for the Czech underground to be able to come to our rescue. It feels good to have a purpose and be part of this group. The Czechs agree to deliver weapons, including a machine gun supported by a tripod, to Schindler. It's the best they can do for us now.

In December, a member of my underground group awakens me in bed. He whispers in my ear to go immediately to Schindler's room to receive something from him and to bring it directly to the kitchen. He hurries away after he gives me the instructions.

Fully awake now, my attention to details takes over. Schindler and his wife, Emilie, never sleep in their comfortable villa at Brunnlitz. Bless them. They sleep in a small room at the factory because Schindler knows we Jews are afraid of late night visits from the SS.

I grab the heavy gray blanket I sleep under and drape it over my head. For anyone who watches me, I am supposedly going downstairs to the latrine. Instead, I head outside to the barracks building. The Schindlers' room is located in back of the factory at one end of the factory hall.

My senses on high alert, I knock lightly on the door. There's minimal light.

"*Ist dat Jozek?*" Is that Jozek?

"*Jawohl.*" Yes.

I recognize Schindler's voice but can't see his face as he partially opens the door. He extends from his hands a rifle and a box of ammunition. I conceal them under my blanket. I hurry to the kitchen door and knock lightly. The door opens only wide enough for me to hand the rifle and box of ammunition to the unseen underground member.

The kitchen has six, brown four-feet-tall kettles. Each kettle is the size of a card table. The kettles are hung over beds of hot coals where workers cook soup. The Germans were told one kettle needs repair. Because of Schindler, they let it go without punishing anyone. I am aware the kitchen workers have dug a hole under the kettle that is supposedly not working. This is where I suspect the prisoner will camouflage the rifle and ammunition I handed over to him.

Prisoner workers in the kitchen have served at one time or another in the Polish army. They're capable of handling and firing weapons. Except for the kitchen people, prisoners are counted each morning in the plaza. Kitchen workers are counted in the kitchen.

Our underground is cognizant that whenever Germans have an *Aktion*, the underground will issue an order for the kitchen prisoners to come to the plaza. This will be the signal for the underground not to go. We will fight!

I'm nervous as I walk back from the factory to the sleeping quarters. My heartbeat accelerates like the banging on a drum, beating harder and harder against my chest.

I start to relax when I enter the sleeping quarters. I pass the approximate fourteen inches by fourteen inches hole hidden in the wall connected to the women's quarters. It's through this hole that men and women talk to one another in the evening. I uncover the blanket from my head and collapse on a straw mattress on a wooden bunk. Job done. Schindler is a good man.

December of 1944 runs into January of 1945. I'm still laboring at installing an electric-wire fence around the factory camp. The frigid weather attacks my body. I rub my frozen hands together and stamp my numb feet. My stomach groans for more food.

I push a wheelbarrow to carry wire from one of the storage buildings. The buildings consist of similar rows of single-car garages. In addition to the wire, potatoes, canned food, and pork are housed there, mostly for the guards.

There's a truckload of potatoes being unloaded in the middle of the plaza. An SS guard armed with a submachine gun stands by the truck. I make a split-second decision. When the guard turns his back away from me, I rush to the truck, grab two potatoes, put them inside the wheelbarrow and continue on to the storeroom. I conceal the potatoes underneath the wire.

Not far from the job site, I stoop down, dig a hole in the frozen dirt, and light a match to twigs and pieces of wood. I work fast. As the potatoes begin to bake, I proceed to my assignment with the wire in the wheelbarrow. I savor the thought of eating the potatoes.

Soon after I reach the area, a German guard arrives to inspect the work on the fence. He notices smoke from the fire and kicks the ground open. He sees the potatoes. I'm working away from the hole where the potatoes are baking.

The guard barks at us, "Who put the potatoes there. Whoever put the potatoes in the ground, report to me immediately!"

What should I do? Stay quiet? What if we all get punished? My impulsive act leaves me with no choice. I can't jeopardize everyone else.

I tell the guard I'm the guilty party. Bad timing. Why did he have to be here now? The guard beats my back with the butt of his rifle and makes me run around in circles. My hunger pains are replaced with the loss of strength in my body. My punishment doesn't end here. The guard forbids me to get soup for two weeks. Bastard.

That afternoon, the guard commands me to go through the food line with my metal cup and turn the cup over when I get to the soup pot. Coffee is served in the barracks in the morning, bread in the evening. Soup is served in the open in the afternoon. It's easy for the guard to control.

I get lucky. I don't know who gives the order, but an underground member who works in the kitchen delivers good soup to me in my barracks that evening. The soup has some slivers of potatoes from the bottom of the pot. It quiets my hunger pains. The guard watches me move through the line and turn my cup over for the next two weeks. Ha, if he only knew. I'm getting better food than I did before. I continue to get soup in the barracks.

With the fence completed, I am assigned to work inside the factory. My job is to install new machinery for use in making weapons. What a relief to work out of the brutal cold. The factory is in operation twenty-four hours a day. My shift is eleven hours. Schindler walks through the factory in the mornings and stops at every machine. He chain-smokes on the factory floor. He greets us, lights a German cigarette, and places it next to each prisoner's hand. He treats us like humans.

Once the machinery is installed and functioning, my assignment is to work on it. There are several stages of processing the weapons. We start with a block of metal that is drawn and tapered to a very sharp point. The next stage of production is to put it into metal softening, annealing ovens, and oversee the ovens that are a part of the ammunition manufacturing process. Then the weapon is sent to another factory so that an additional part can be added for final assembling.

Rumor circulates in the factory that Schindler has changed the drawing by modifying the screw thread so that it does not match up with the part in the other factory. Therefore, the weapon cannot be assembled. The antitank weapon tip I am producing is worthless!

Early 1945, Schindler takes some Jewish workers with him in a large truck to two railroad cars full of Jewish prisoners. The railroad cars hold about three hundred prisoners, almost all of them frozen to death. The workers are able to remove about forty prisoners still alive. Workers put the ill prisoners on Schindler's truck to be taken back to the factory. Schindler and his wife care for the prisoners who are set up in an unused hall. Within a few weeks they are well enough to be assigned to the factory. Schindler and his wife are good people.

The factory underground puts the word out to the prisoners that Schindler is running out of money. He needs valuables to help pay off the SS and to aid us. We are told that if anyone has any valuables, we should give them to him.

I still have the five-dollar gold-coin I had taped to the bottom of my foot before going into the showers at Gross-Rosen. I would have had a second gold-coin if Wilus hadn't been so careless and lost it in the showers.

I decide to give the coin to Schindler. I'm not doing it because I'm a nice guy. I'm doing it because it's for my life.

There is a man, Mr. Schweber, who is in daily contact with Schindler. I tell him about the gold coin. He arranges for me to go with him and meet with Schindler. We go to Schindler's office, and I personally hand the coin over to him.

He shakes my hand. "Jozek, thank you. You will get an extra bread until the war ends."

At my next meal, I receive a whole loaf of bread. My hunger pains subside only to start up again when I do not receive any more extra bread. Such is life. I'm glad I gave him the gold-coin anyway.

During this time, Russian armies are moving in from the east. The Nazis are starting to liquidate more of the occupied concentration camps in Poland. We hear through the underground that the Nazis are forcibly marching all inmates west.

Although I do not live in a heightened state of fear for myself, I'm terribly worried about what dangers Mamusia, Manek, and Sabcia are facing. I have no information about them. I fervently hope they are alive. They have to be.

My worry doesn't stop there. I worry about Hanka and her mother. I consider how things would be different if they were on the transport with the other women who came to Schindler's factory. I'd be able to see Hanka, to talk to her, and most of all I would know she and her mother are safe. They are prisoners in Auschwitz with no defense against outbursts of the Germans' vile attacks. It's labeled a death camp. Are Hanka and her mother even still there? They must be strong enough to resist the German brutality.

I'm also anxious about Leon, Roman, and Wilus who were forced to leave Schindler's factory and go to Auschwitz. If only Schindler was here when they were ordered to leave, he would have saved them. Do they see Hanka and her mother at Auschwtiz? I know nothing.

The unknown is frightening. Having no control of my life is terrible. Schindler's factory is a safe place, but I'm still a prisoner. I'm without resources to help anyone.

From Captivity to Liberation

Chapter 25

November 1944 to January 1945 – I Should Not Have Screamed

Roman

We are being treated okay. Tatus, Wilus, and I sit on wooden benches in a third-class wagon of the Polish State Railroad along with the other fathers and sons who were ordered by the Germans to leave Schindler's factory.

We're almost like typical passengers, except we're not. SS guards, a sergeant and a corporal, escort us. They carry rifles. Other travelers try to avoid looking at us through their hateful faces.

What did the Jews ever do to them? We've never harmed anyone. Nothing I can do to change their evil minds. I breathe in some clean fresh air.

I whisper to Wilus, "The officer is not a bad man. He gave us something to eat from the cafeteria when the train stopped at the train station. It's a long time since we ate sandwiches. It has stopped the rumblings in my stomach."

"We are going to Auschwitz. It's in Oswiecim, Poland. People get killed there. But don't worry, Wilus, if the Nazis wanted to kill us, we would be dead already."

"I know."

"If Schindler was at the factory, he would have stopped the Germans from making us leave."

"I know."

"Okay, smarty, you know everything."

"Some things."

This place is huge. There are watchtowers and electrified fences with double-barbed wire as far as I can see in the distance. I point out the sign over the main entrance to Wilus, *Arbeit macht*

frei, Work makes free. Who are they kidding? Working doesn't help. The hard labor makes people drop dead.

There are rows of barracks housed in red brick buildings. We are taken to one of the barracks and put into a separate section for the night. We try to sleep on a blanket on a cold floor. This place is a lot worse than Plaszow and nothing like Schindler's factory. It's another place, different people. Prisoners look like men in striped pajamas.

Repeated gunfire shots break the quiet of the night. A prisoner from across the barracks calls out that Russian prisoners are being shot at a place called the Black Wall of Death. He says their bodies are put into mass graves. What will happen to us here?

The next day guards walk the fathers and boys transported from Schindler's factory on unpaved roads to Auschwitz II, called Birkenau. It takes us almost an hour until we walk into a hall next to a big hole.

We are ordered to undress. Shit! I can't believe it. When we undress, we see what we thought was a boy is really a girl. She has a flat chest and short hair. She is seized by the guards and taken away. What will they do to her? She must be very smart to have gotten this far. I hope she can talk her way out of getting killed.

Guards take us to the showers to delouse us and to shave our heads. They give us clothing: pants, short sleeve shirts, and shoes - but no socks or underwear. I keep thinking about that brazen girl. She has guts. I wish I could have spoken with her.

We're ordered to line up to get a tattoo. I hear one of the prisoners say it's so the Germans can call us by number. I know why they want to call us by number. It's to belittle us and take away our identity. I line up in back of Tatus. Wilus stands behind me.

When my turn comes, I am branded with blue numbers etched into my left forearm by searing metal rods. I scream at the pain. Blood jumps out. My body shakes. I extend my arm and read my number, B14435.

Wilus cries before they even tattoo him. I should not have screamed, but it hurts like hell. Wilus' number is after mine, B14436. Tatus says we're lucky because we have numbers. He says numbers mean we will live. I do my best to suck in the pain and advise Wilus to do the same. "Don't be a crybaby."

"I'm not a crybaby," he complains. He holds his forearm and tries to blink away his tears. I shouldn't be rough on him. He's trying to be brave.

After we're tattooed, Wilus and I are forced to separate from Tatus. I don't want to leave him. Why are they doing this? The Germans are taking boys and their fathers to different barracks.

Before we leave Tatus, he hugs Wilus and me and says we will be okay, but I see his face tight with worry. He tells me not to do anything to call attention to us, to be invisible to the guards.

Why can't we stay together? I don't want to go. I hold onto Tatus too long. A German guard yells at us to separate and points to Wilus and me to join with the other children.

Chapter 26

They Make Us Stand Like Scarecrows

Roman

Wilus and I step onto a filthy damp muddy floor. We're put into the barracks with other young prisoners. They have blank expressionless faces on their skinny bodies. They look like skeletons covered with sores from scratching lice. The barracks' supervisor, a *kapo*, calls out our tattooed numbers. We're told to go into the wooden bunks having three or four tiers.

Wilus climbs in first. I squeeze in next to him. There's a thin straw sack on the shelves. Prisoners give out strong odors of sweat, fatigue, and fear. It stinks here.

Wilus and I pull at the blanket infected with lice to cover us. It's so thin it doesn't give us any warmth. I caution Wilus to be quiet and get some sleep. I tell him I'll stay awake, alert for whatever happens next. Wilus falls asleep right away.

A few days later, an unbelievable thing takes place at Birkenau. The barracks is located against the barbed-wire fence of the women's camp. When Wilus and I come out of our barracks and look through the wire fence, we can't believe it. We see Mamusia and Hanka. Their heads are shaved. They look strange without their hair.

"Hanka! Mamusia! Why aren't you at Schindler's?" I shout to them.

"We were taken off of the list," my sister answers as she and Mamusia rush to the fence.

"You went to Schindler's. Why are you both here?" Hanka asks.

"The Germans made us leave because we're too young to work on the machinery. Tatus came with us. Schindler was away."

"Tatus, here?" my sister asks.

"Where? Where is Leon?" Mamusia asks.

"Tatus is in another barracks."

Hanka wants to know how Jozek is withstanding the imprisonment. I tell her Schindler's factory is a good place. Safe.

"Thank G-d you're all alive. I prayed you would be safe, but I thought you were at Schindler's factory. Jozek is lucky. This camp is atrocious," my sister says.

"Mamusia and I try keeping our bodies clean by rubbing them with hands full of snow. I bite my lip until it bleeds and rub the blood on Mamusia's and my cheeks to give us color so we don't look sick."

Hanka cautions me to watch out for Dr. Mengele. He performs experiments on children. He's a dangerous man. She tells us to hide from him. Now I have an extra thing to worry about. Wilus is a good-looking kid.

Hanka says our cousin Rena and her mother are at Schindler's factory with other women who were on the list. I explain they must have come after we left. We didn't see them.

Three days later Mamusia and Hanka are transported out of Auschwitz-Birkenau. Wilus and I have no idea where they were relocated. They were never able to see Tatus. I'm scared for them.

Shootings take place all night. Prisoners are shot in their barracks. I hear guards yelling and loud noises. Shrieking air-raid sirens go off and on. German guards shout at us to get in line. They herd us out of the barracks with whips, like cattle, for roll call. Germans jab us in our ribs with their rifles and force us to stand in bitter cold.

They make us stand like scarecrows and use us like human shields in a cornfield. Germans want the allied bombers to see us so they won't fire at them. We have to stay in one place. Prisoners who fall down are shot. I stand in line next to Wilus as still and as straight as I can, but I can't stop shivering. I hate the freezing cold. Wilus and I stick our hands in our mouths to try to warm them. It doesn't help.

I was able to arrange with a *kapo* for me and some other kids to collect garbage and put it into wagons. When I come to the kitchen, I steal food and put garbage on top of it. Adults in the camp take care of Wilus when I am away. I give them food for watching him.

Chapter 27

We Walk in Blinding Snow

Roman

Loud speakers blast orders instructing us to vacate the Auschwitz-Birkenau concentration camp's barracks. Wilus and I rush out with other children to assemble on the *Appellplatz* for the roll call count. Bitter cold slices into our skin. We stumble on the ice and snow blanketing the ground. The SS call out the blue branded tattooed numbers on our inner left arms. Wilus and I violently shiver standing in the children's line.

Is it the frost or fear that makes us shiver so much? Could it be the uncertainty of the purpose of the lineup? This feels different. The Germans are overly anxious to quickly get the count done. Are we going to be killed?

Women empty their barracks and huddle together in rows near us. After the count, the SS order us to march to the Auschwitz roll call area. My heart is racing. I feel the sting of Wilus' cold breath on my back. The Germans will shoot us if we don't march in step.

They shout we are being transported by freight trains to other concentration camps. But I know the real reason. They want to prevent the advancing Russian army from seeing starved and dying prisoners. They don't want witnesses to their criminal acts. What concentration camps will we be sent to? Will Tatus go with us?

When the Germans split Tatus from Wilus and me, he was commanded to go into a separate barracks for men. Standing on my toes, stretching my neck, and searching across prisoner lines, I'm lucky. I find Tatus.

"Quick. Wilus. Come. I see Tatus in his barracks' line."

We peel off from the children's lines. "Keep your head down because we don't want the Germans to see us."

Tatus' drained face manages a smile when we reach him. He grabs Wilus and me into his arms. I loosen myself from his grip and look into his dark puffy eyes. I make a quick decision.

"Tatus, I'm not going to march."

"What do you mean you are not going to march? Where will you go?"

"I'll find a hiding place."

"Roman. No. Listen. You must march with me. We'll be together."

"I can't. I'm sorry, Tatus."

I pull Wilus by his hand. We cut away, dodging inmates who look like ghostly gray scarecrows. I caution Wilus to keep my pace and not to look at anyone.

British bombers are flying over the camp. Because of our small size, we're able to dart unnoticed by the Germans, in and out of the prisoners' lines. I feel terrible leaving Tatus. It agitates me that I can't help him. I'm scared for him and also for Wilus and me. Where should we go? I raise my head to look above the lines for a place to hide. I see a few kids running.

"Wilus, run with me to those kids." I motion with my right hand to the kids running straight ahead of us.

"Shouldn't we go back and march with your father?"

Wilus hesitates and stays in place. He's young. He doesn't know anything. "No. Move!"

We catch up on the heels of the other children pressing through prisoners' lines. Like us, they're seeking a way to escape from the march. I realize they're headed to the barracks' alley leading to the Germans' barracks. No one is in sight. No one stops us. No time to think of a safer place to hide.

Are we crazy to go into the Germans' barracks? There are two entrances. On one side of the buildings, the Germans are packing up to evacuate the camp and accompany the prisoners. We all dash to the other side.

Inside the brick barracks is a pantry full of cans of food. Shit! A can of beef tumbles out of my hands and hits my left arm. I rub my throbbing arm for a few seconds before grasping cans of meats and German bread. Wilus begins to eat from cans of fruits and meats.

The food eases our hunger pains, but we need to get out of here. We can't risk being found. The Germans will shoot us on the spot. Shortly after we have our fill of food, I tell Wilus we must leave, that I'm frightened and don't feel safe here.

"No. Let's stay. I don't want to go outside. It's cold. We have food. The other kids aren't leaving."

"Stop whining, Wilus. I say we are leaving. Let's go."

"No!"

He tries to yank his arm away from me. I try reasoning with him, but I don't have much time.

"Wilus, do you want to get shot? We're in the Germans' barracks. They could come back."

I don't wait for an answer. I pull him with me to the door. A swish of cold air crashes into my body when I open it. Violent shivers strike our bodies. Snow has begun falling. The alley is quiet and free of Germans as far as I can see.

"Come on. We're going now." My cousin Wilus is an eight-year-old kid. I'm eleven and the decision maker here.

Heavy gusts of thick snow smack us when we step outside.

"See. I said we should stay."

"Quiet! We have to leave. It's not safe to stay in the Germans' barracks. I told you they could come back and kill us."

We walk in blinding snow. We see a blood red sky on the horizon. It's a sure sign fighting is close. Russians are coming from the east. British, French, and Americans are coming from the west.

I say we should walk toward the bleeding sky. Wilus reluctantly nods his head in agreement. I don't know if I can do this. The weather may kill us if the Nazis don't. I falter in the snow only to feel Wilus pulling on my hand urging me to walk faster.

The Auschwitz electrical station is in our sight. I know the prisoner, Mr. Ginter, who was the station's electrical engineer. He and his son went to Schindler's factory with us. They were forced to leave the factory along with Tatus, Wilus, me, and the other fathers and their sons. They must be marching out of Auschwitz like Tatus.

Discovered. I'll never forget the day the Germans found all the children in the factory and called for our fathers to depart with us. Tatus claimed Wilus as his responsibility.

Bad luck for us that Schindler was away. We were transported to Auschwitz-Birkenau because we were too young to work on the machinery. If Schindler were there, he would have stopped them. He would have found a way, insisted we were important to the war effort. He would have made up jobs for us. He would have saved us.

The Germans found Wilus and me playing among the abandoned spinning machines. If only we had been given some warning, I would have found a place for us to hide until Schindler came back. Tatus would have been safe. He wouldn't have had to leave the factory. He wouldn't be on the march.

Wilus insists we take cover in the electrical station. We are cold and wet from snow slapping our bodies.

I give in. He's more like a brother to me than a cousin. I have to take care of him.

"We'll go in," I say, "but we're not staying long." He gives me that smile of his where his hazel eyes turn to blue and light up. He's a cute kid.

We dig away a pile of snow with our stiff hands and stamp our feet to flatten out the snow. We lean together and shove the door open. There's no heat in the brick building. A quilt on a small bed helps a little to dry us and stop the shivers. We sleep on the bed at night trying to catch some warmth from the closeness of our bodies. I dream of Tatus telling me everything will be okay. That thought escapes me when I awake.

In the morning, we walk around rubbing our hands together to stop them from going numb. After two and a half days of this, I decide I've had enough. It's time to leave. It takes pushing on the door, back and forth, to open it wide enough for us to squeeze through.

We walk in blinding swirling snow white as milk, two small phantasms. Huge snowdrifts blur our vision. Thin worn clothing is our only protection against the frigid cold. We have no socks, no underwear. Our shoes are soaked. Our toes, fingers, and ears are numb. Wilus keeps sinking into the snow. I keep yanking him out. We trudge along until Auschwitz is in our sight. We have circled back.

What will we find inside the camp? It's almost impossible to maneuver with the snowdrifts and the snow. I have no good choices. I make the decision to go back inside the concentration camp. The place looks deserted of the German guards. We have to be careful none of them are left. Heavy gunfire thunders from a distance.

Chapter 28

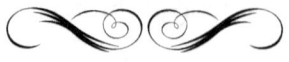

He Is Only a Boy

Wilus

The afternoon of January 27, 1945, Russian soldiers are liberating us at Auschwitz. Roman just had his twelfth birthday. I'm eight-years-old. I'll be nine in a few months.

Roman went to stand behind the barbed-wire fence with other prisoners to see the Russians coming into the camp. His left arm is bandaged. He got hurt from toppling the cans in the barracks' pantry when we escaped from the Germans and the march.

I'm in the barracks' basement standing on a box and peering out of the basement window. I can see what's going on. The Russians are staring back at the prisoners at the fence. I see an officer on skis come in behind the tanks. I'm glad I didn't go with Roman. It's freezing outside. There's snow on the ground.

We are free. We no longer have to be afraid the Germans will kill us. A Russian wearing a fur cap is riding in a horse-drawn sled in the street. He passes by the basement window where I'm standing. He is only a boy! He has smooth skin. He has no beard.

Sick prisoners who couldn't march with the other inmates when they had the forced march out of Auschwitz are dropping dead around us. Roman wants us to walk toward Krakow to look for his parents, sister, and Jozek. I want to find them too. They are my only family. I have no one else.

Roman and I are dressed in our worn clothing: pants, long sleeve shirts, and jackets. I'm wearing the striped prisoners' cap. Roman and I hold hands and walk out into the deep snow.

Chapter 29

November 1944 to April 1945 – I Fought Back Like a Crazy Woman

Hanka

It's November 1944. Mamusia and I are squeezed into the cattle car with other prisoners. This transport from Auschwitz-Birkenau to another camp is taking a long time.

Things happened fast. We saw Roman and Wilus at Birkenau but never got to see Tatus. Are they going to be transferred out of the concentration camp like Mamusia and me? Jozek is safe at Schindler's factory. What will happen to the rest of us? I need to take care of Mamusia.

We hear bombardments. I can't see through the small window with bars near the top of the cattle car. I tell Mamusia sounds of bombardments are a good sign. The war will end soon.

Mamusia is sitting on scattered straw on the floor of the cattle car. I am standing near her. The stink from the overflowing bucket where people do their business stings my eyes. I try concentrating on better times. *I play outside the farmhouse in the fresh air of summer. The sky is blue. The sun embraces my body.*

Auschwitz was hell. The SS men and women sorted us out as soon as we stumbled out of the boxcar from Plaszow. Dogs barked. German guards marched us, our feet sticking in the mud, to have our hair shaved.

We had heard about the gas chambers and that some shower nozzles had a killing gas. My body trembled when Mamusia and I were hurried into the showers with rows and rows of showerheads. There was no way to resist. We clung to each other. I knew we were alive when icy-water pricked our bodies. I kissed Mamusia on her forehead. We gave thanks to G-d.

After the showers, we were ushered into a room to take dead prisoners' clothes and a pair of wooden clogs. Next we were taken to a barracks in the women's camp. We stepped on a cold, clay floor. Mamusia and I slept on thin straw pallets with ragged wet blankets. For the first three and a half weeks, we slept on separate shelves in the barracks. The older women slept on the bottom shelves, and the younger women took the top shelves.

We knew something was wrong when we didn't go straight to the factory, but we thought Schindler would rescue us when we didn't arrive. Mamusia and I were horrified to learn our names were no longer on Schindler's List. We were not going to the factory. We were no longer going to be saved. We were taken to a women's camp in Birkenau. Nothing can be worse than Auschwitz-Birkenau.

Wrong. Wrong. I'm wrong. We were transported to Bergen-Belsen. It's worse. Bergen-Belsen is near the villages of Bergen and Belsen in northern Germany. It's about 16 kilometers, 10 miles, northwest of Celle, Germany. It was once used as an exchange camp where Jewish prisoners were exchanged for detained Germans.

Mamusia and I are in this camp now for almost five months. There are no gas chambers, but things are horrible just the same. The women's compound is large and overcrowded. We try to keep it clean. Parts of skeletal corpses lie around outside the barracks.

There is a typhus epidemic in camp. Mamusia got diarrhea first, then typhus. I have typhus too. I'm feverish and tired, but I can stand on my feet. I need to gather my strength. Mamusia feels hot to the touch. Food is scarce. Lice are everywhere. They stick to our bodies and to our clothes. My scalp itches. I do the best I can to pick the lice off of Mamusia and me.

I still have Jozek's identity card photo that he gave me when we were separated at Plaszow. I miss him. Thinking about seeing him gives me strength. A German guard tried to take his photo from me. I wouldn't give it to her, not even when she beat my shoulders and back with a whip. I don't know what came over me, but I fought back like a crazy woman.

I would not let go of his picture. It was the only thing I had that was mine. In all the misery, I found love. I was not going to let the Germans take this away from me. Finally the guard gave up and stopped beating me.

Gone. Gone is my life as I knew it. My youth slips away. I try hiding my fears for Mamusia's sake, but they are there inside me. I cannot think into the future. I can think only about one day at a time.

I want to close my eyes in my own bed, not worry about lice climbing onto my body. Prisoners say the war will end soon. I want to believe this. Mamusia and I must not become skeletons like other prisoner.

The Allied 21st Army Group, a combined British-Canadian unit, liberates us on April 15, 1945.

We were without food and water for several days. Because of typhus and other illnesses in the camp, the British wait for the medical corps to come to our aid while they detour around the camp. Air raid alarms shriek. Buildings burn. The British want to stop the typhus from spreading.

There are random shootings by some German guards as they leave. They are the ones who should be shot. At last it's quiet. The Nazis are gone. We are safe.

The British army distributes food and water. I hold onto Mamusia and hug her bony body. Tears crowd our thin faces. We cry happy tears that we are alive and triumphed over evil. We want to let go of the horrific unimaginable things that were done to us to come to this day. We mourn those who were killed. We hold onto the wonderful thought that we will see Tatus, Roman, Jozek, and Wilus again.

Chapter 30

1944 to 1945 – The Order is a Fake

Jozek

I know nothing about Leon, Roman, and Wilus since they were forced to leave for Auschwitz with the other boys and their fathers. Do they see Hanka and her mother? I will myself to hold onto the belief they, as well as, Mamusia, Sabcia and Manek, are all alive.

I am energized being a part of the camp's underground group. My spirits are lifted knowing I can help in some way. A piece of paper with instructions to participate in an *Aktion* is to be hidden under my machinery by an underground member. Each day I search to see if there's an order for me.

The first one arrives. The Czech underground wants a count of German guards in the camp. Electricians in the underground are singled out for this job. The underground need us to produce an electrical outage in the Germans' barracks. The Germans will have to call electricians to come and restore the power. It's not an unusual occurrence. There will be no reason for them to suspect we were the cause of their loss of electricity.

A prisoner who is an authentic electrician creates the short. Lights go out. Guards summon us to check their loss of power. When we come to their barracks, the German guards leave us to do our work. We count beds. Next to each bed is a closet. We make an assumption if there is an empty open closet then no one sleeps in that bed. We look for a pair of shoes in the closet thinking someone occupies the bed next to the closet. If the bed is too neat, we decide no German guard sleeps there. We check two huge table drawers next to the bed.

None of our totals is precise. We look over our shoulders as we count, unsure if any of the Germans will come back. What should I say if a German confronts me? I'll answer I'm restoring the electricity. What if he asks why I'm looking at beds? I'll answer I'm looking for a loose wire. I'm on an adrenaline rush. Fear is a constant companion. Sweat fills my armpits, behind my neck, and across my forehead.

When our count is done, a signal is given to restore the power. Eventually, German guards receive an order for the fifty youngest guards to report to a city in Russia, more than 160 kilometers east, 100 miles. The older guards are to stay in the camp. I watch the commandant count out the younger guards, load them onto a truck, and take them out of the camp.

The order is a fake! The underground issued the order. We don't know for sure if the guards ever made it to the Russian front. I very much doubt it.

The SS officer in charge of our camp has been reassigned to another camp. Luck is with me. We find out the commandant ordered the Germans to dig graves for us in the forest. Now with him gone, with the young guards away on the truck, there's no one who will give the command to shoot us.

Meanwhile, Russian armies are moving in from the east. The Germans have liquidated most of the concentration camps in Nazi-Occupied Poland. The Germans are forcibly marching all the inmates to the west. During these marches, in the winter of 1944 into 1945, many thousands of prisoners are killed or die of starvation and exhaustion. I need to be strong. It's close to the end. I can feel it.

Oscar Schindler has loudspeakers installed all over the factory for us to hear news from the BBC in London. I help to connect two speakers to the German Blaupunkt radio. The broadcast says the war is coming to an end.

May 7, 1945, the BBC reports Germany's surrender. The war in Europe is to cease at midnight the following night. We keep to our usual routines. Excitement in the air is contagious.

Free. We are to be free. I have so many thoughts going through my head about seeing Mamusia, Manek, Sabcia, Hanka, Malia, Leon, Roman, and Wilus. I am alive! They must be alive! I mustn't dwell on negative thoughts.

At noon, Schindler pipes in Prime Minister Winston Churchill's victory speech by loudspeaker that's heard throughout the camp. As Schindler walks onto the factory floor, all eyes are upon him. He directs a speech to the remaining armed SS guards assembled in the factory. He tells them he knows they were given orders to kill all prisoners before the end of the war. Schindler says they must decide whether they will go home as murderers or join their families and live their lives in peace. His words are powerful.

The SS look confused. Their orders were to kill the Jews. Schindler also cautions prisoners to refrain from acts of revenge and terror. After listening to his intense words, the SS decide to leave us alone. We are happy about this, but our prisoner underground is prepared to use weapons from the Czech underground to confront the SS.

Before Schindler ends his speech, he asks everyone to keep a three-minute silence in memory of the victims who had died. I lower my head and silently say the Mourner's Kaddish for my father, Abraham, and brother, Milek. I add a prayer for Hanka's brother, Manek, and Wilus' parents, Frania and Henryk.

The SS obey Schindler. After his speech, the Germans begin to leave the hall and give up their weapons. Damn them. They are the lucky ones. They get to go home to their families.

On Tuesday, May 8, 1945, Germany has capitulated. The war has ended. I feel as if a heavy weight has been lifted off of my body and my soul.

Schindler opens a storeroom and distributes several pieces of fabric to the prisoners with which we can use to barter with or make something out of it. We also receive underwear, a bottle of vodka, and a ration of Egipski cigarettes.

Schindler and his wife, Emilie, leave the factory dressed in the prisoners' striped uniforms, which they will take off once they reach the American-Occupied zones in Austria and Germany. Some prisoners, wearing their camp clothing, volunteer to travel with them in Schindler's Mercedes. Other prisoners follow Schindler and his wife in a truck loaded with food, liquor, and cigarettes, for bartering along the way.

I help load their possessions into the truck and watch Schindler and his wife leave the factory. He saved my life. Schindler has with him a letter signed by some prisoners attesting to his and his wife's records of looking after his prisoners. They must have saved over a thousand Jewish lives.

For weeks after they leave, the underground, twenty-eight people including me, control the factory. Schindler's camp has a warehouse with canned food and prisoners break into the warehouse. We now have food to eat.

Since we are over 160 kilometers, 100 miles, from either front, we're waiting for some authority to arrive to tell us what to do. The factory is on the right side of a main road. We see Germans on the road as they try to flee from the Russian front to the Americans. Some are in cars, others on horses.

The Germans don't want to fall into Russian hands. They expect they will be brutally treated in return for what they did to the Russians. They want to become American prisoners of war. Russians control the eastern front, the Americans and British the western front.

We have weapons: nine rifles, ten handguns, and a machine gun from Schindler to defend ourselves. We put the machine gun on the roof and place the weapon facing down in position to be fired. I stand on the road with other underground members.

As Germans approach, we point our guns at them and say, "Drop your weapons, strip to your underwear." We will allow them to go west on foot in their underwear. Weather is not a factor, as it has been so many times for us, because it's the month of May. We don't shoot at the Germans when we see them because they have weapons and can fight back.

But we have leverage. They quickly calm down and drop their weapons when they see we're ready to pull the trigger of the machine gun on the roof. They obey our orders, undress, and walk away. It feels good to finally be in a position of power.

Now that the war has ended, the rule is Germans are not to have any weapons. We put their confiscated weapons and uniforms into a huge room.

One day while we are defending Schindler's factory, SS soldiers on motorcycles come to the gate of the camp. They request to see Mr. Schindler. The soldiers want to obtain plans of the weapons he was building. Who are they to demand anything? Don't they know who the winner is here?

Some of the twenty-eight people in charge are in the guardhouse. The leader of our group is at the gate. He informs them Mr. Schindler is not here and no documents will be given. With rifles pointed at them by people in the guardhouse, the underground leader instructs the SS to drop their weapons. They have no choice if they want to live. They drop their weapons.

Then one of the SS soldiers tells our leader they are running out of gasoline. He asks him to give them some. Let them walk. We owe them nothing. That's what I would do. But our underground leader allows them to fill their motorcycles with some gasoline. They leave without a fight.

Russians are the first to enter our camp about two weeks after the war ends. Fortunately, there are people from our underground who speak Russian. A lone Russian officer on a horse comes into the camp first and tells us the Russians will occupy this camp within a few days. He says an administrative group will arrive and process us for repatriation back to Krakow.

True to his word in a few days the administrative colonel, who happens to be Jewish and speaks Yiddish, arrives with his subordinates.

We deliver the weapons we have confiscated to him. The colonel is pleased with the large amount of weapons the underground has collected from the Germans. He's instrumental in having the commandant of the Ukrainian front give all twenty-eight of us papers that call us heroes.

The paper says, "All of Russia and the Communist Authority will regard you as a hero of the Russian Republic." The commandant of the Ukrainian front puts his stamp, an unusual triangular stamp, on the paper. These papers are important documents. The colonel tells us the paper will take us anywhere in Russia.

I survived hell. I survived because of luck, and I'm one of the privileged ones to have this piece of paper. Many times, in the constant shadows of death, things could have gone down differently. Now I have this valuable piece of paper. I am free to suck in air without the stench of death, to walk without a gun pointed at my head, and to start thinking of a future.

I savor the sun hitting my face. The gnawing of my stomach quiets. Simple things give me pleasure. I smile and laugh again. I have beaten the odds. I made it out alive. I'm twenty-eight-years-old. It's time to put my life together.

Now I must begin the search for Mamusia, Sabcia, Manek, Hanka, Leon, Malia, Roman, and Wilus. I will not stop until I find them all.

After Liberation and Coming to America

Chapter 31

I Thought All the Jews Were Killed

Roman

A day after we're liberated, Wilus and I meet up with Yasick, a non-Jewish prisoner, who joins us on our way to Krakow. I drag Wilus through the snowdrifts. Yasick drags his bicycle.

We wear thin clothing. We have no warm protection against the freezing weather. Our shoes are drenched, our socks soaked through with snow. Our toes feel numb; our feet have blisters. There are icicles in our pants and down our legs. Wilus doesn't complain. He's a good kid. Nothing we can do but walk on.

Along the way we encounter the Russian front. Soldiers occupying homes welcome us inside to be fed. It's good to come in out of the stinging cold. Food is a welcome relief to rumblings in our stomachs. We make our way as best we can, sleeping in farmhouses, sometimes unknown to the owners.

When we reach Yasick's house, he has a happy reunion with his mother. He invites us to sleep over. At night, I overhear his mother ask him why he brought us here. Then I hear her say, "I thought all the Jews were killed."

Shit, a Nazi sympathizer. The sooner we get out of this house the better. We leave early the next morning. I don't want to stay a minute longer. Wilus and I join up with a group of Jews who are walking outside Yasick's home. It takes four days to reach Krakow, about 60 kilometers, over 40 miles, to the east.

I locate the Jewish relief organization in the city. It gives us a roof over our heads, a place to stay. Daily we ask people if they know anything about my parents, sister, and Jozek. We hear nothing.

I learn that across town Russians have a non-Jewish camp with more food. I decide to take Wilus and go there. We end up being fed in the Russian camp in the evenings. We go back to the Jewish organization's house to sleep and eat during the day. It's a good plan. We are no longer hungry. I am pleased with myself. If I had ever acted as a child, Wilus and I would be dead.

Wilus begins to have earaches. He's in a lot of pain. He can't sleep at night. A doctor at the Jewish relief organization examines his right ear and gives him something for the pain. He has an ear infection and needs to have a mastoid operation. In Plaszow before his parents were murdered, Wilus had a mastoid operation on the same ear.

A man from the relief organization takes Wilus to a Catholic hospital in Warsaw. While Wilus is at the hospital in Warsaw, I recognize a *kapo* on a street in Krakow. He had beaten the hell out of prisoners in Auschwitz. I quickly turn him into the Jewish authorities. His trial is announced over the radio. I'm glad I reported him. He shouldn't get away with what he did to the prisoners in the concentration camp.

Soon after, doctors connected with the Jewish relief organization discover I have a heart murmur. They send me to recuperate, along with about forty or fifty kids, to the Rabka Village in the Carpathian Mountains. This place was a luxurious resort town before the war. We are well fed. It's enjoyable spending my time playing games and soccer. I like being here, but finding my family is my top priority. It's constantly on my mind.

Luckily, Wilus and I were able to escape from the Germans in Auschwitz. Hanka and Mamusia were taken from Auschwitz-Birkenau before they were able to see Tatus. My father was forced to go on the march. Where did they all end up? Jozek should be okay. He must have been liberated at Schindler's factory.

Eventually, I am brought back to the Jewish relief organization on Dluga Street. Wilus is still in the hospital. It was a nice vacation in the mountains. I feel healthy.

At the Jewish home, I meet Mr. Horowitz. He's the relative of the Horowitzes who lived with us in the Krakow suburbs and the Podgorze ghetto. Mr. Horowitz is still in the funeral business. He's in charge of the Jewish cemetery committee and is the cemetery caretaker.

In early August, I travel by myself on a trolley car to visit him at the cemetery. I hear screams, "Beat the Jews!" from outside the trolley car. I stare out of the moving trolley car window and see people chasing and hitting Jews. The *AK Armja Krajowa*, Polish Army, and the Russians who stand along the street are doing nothing to stop the beatings. It's a pogrom! They could come after me.

Frightened, I jump off of the trolley at the next stop and cautiously make my way on foot to Mr. Horowitz. I tell him about the pogrom, and he hides me in the cemetery. Mr. Horowitz says there are also pogroms going on in other cities and towns. The Poles didn't want to give back to the Jews their homes, businesses, and belongings that the Nazis forced us to leave behind when they incarcerated us. The defeat of the Nazis didn't put a stop to their anti-Semitism.

Chapter 32

1945 - I Trust No One

Jozek

The Russians take about a month to process and transport us from Schindler's factory to Krakow. We go back on an overcrowded train, squeezed in tight. We are free. I can tolerate the bodies slammed against me.

Where is my family? Where are Hanka and her family? My mind circles on how I will find them.

In Krakow, the Jewish committee gives us permission to live in a dormitory of a Jewish academic house. I sell the fabric from Schindler's factory for twenty American dollars.

Daily I join others and go to the Krakow Jewish Federation office. Crowds of people push and shove to get to a large wooden table in the middle of the room or to a section of the wall. Situated on the wall and table are lists of people who were at various concentration camps. We search for our families and loved ones. We look for anyone who might know of them.

I learn the painful truth. Germans killed my mother, sister, brother, and forty-two members of my family. I already knew that my older brother, Milek, had been killed in 1942 in Kiev, Russia. Mamusia was transported out of the ghetto in June of 1942 and killed in Belzec, Poland. Sabcia was killed in 1944 in Stutthof, Germany. Manek was killed in 1944 in Mauthausen, Austria.

It's very painful to think back to the wonderful times spent with my family. Now they are all gone: Tatus, Mamusia, Milek, Manek, and Sabcia. One day you have a loving family who plays by the rules and do no harm to anyone. Now I'm left with nothing but memories blackened by thoughts of what their last hours on earth must have been like.

Time after time, I leave the Federation office with no news about Hanka and her family. I envy others who find members of their families. I was powerless to save mine. Although I know I shouldn't, I feel some guilt that somehow I let them down. I grow resentful. How can anyone pray to G-d? These were innocent people. They did not deserve to die this way. I'm bitter.

There comes a point when there are no new lists coming into the office. My friends and I realize we need to make a change. The Communist party's way of life is not for us. We decide to go to the American sector of Austria.

Viktor, my friend who asked me to join the underground group, was Regina Steiner's boyfriend in Krakow before the war. Regina was liberated from Theresienstadt, and they were reunited in Krakow. Viktor and Regina get married in a rabbi's home the day before they leave with us to Austria.

Our group, seven men and four women, moves out of Communist Poland and heads for the Austria Displaced Persons camp controlled by the Americans. Austria is divided into four sectors administered by the Russians, Americans, French, and British. Displaced persons camps were established because most Jews had no homes to return to. Nazi sympathizers attacked Jews who wished to go back to their communities.

The paper with the triangular stamp helps to get us across the borders. Viktor has one of the papers too. We reach the American part of Austria with no trouble. We are given places in the Army barracks, a red brick two-story building, in which seven people sleep in the same room.

Life goes on. Simple things give me pleasure. I keep roasted nuts in my pants pocket that remind me of Mamusia. I have the liberty of movement, of experiencing the freedom to make my own decisions. But I'm not the same carefree Jozek as before the war. I'm on my guard to any situation that might arise. I trust no one.

I take great pleasure in playing cards for money. I sit for hours at the poker table with steeple fingers against my lips, elbows folded against my body. One day I win a suitcase full of Russian money. The suitcase becomes my chair and my pillow. I even take it with me into the bathroom. Eventually, I change the money on the black market into American dollars. Russian money has very little value.

There comes a time when Viktor and I agree we cannot go on like this. We need to do something concrete with our lives. We can't sit around and play cards all the time. We decide to become partners to smuggle merchandise. Lots of people are doing this in some kind of manner.

At the beginning, I was able to cross the borders to get to Poland by showing the Russian paper. But little by little, the borders have become more organized. They are more difficult to get across.

Usually, I take two men who work for Viktor and me to Krakow. The men carry electric motors and whatever else we can find. We lift merchandise from the American warehouses. We get good at this by going into the warehouses at night where there are no security guards. We disassemble fuse boxes and anything else of value, which can be converted into money.

By word of mouth, former prisoners living at the displaced persons camp find out I have this Russian paper and ask to come with me to go from Austria to Poland. One day I take ten people with me. One of my friends has a large suitcase full of shoe leather to sell on the black market.

When we reach the train stop at the Czech and Polish border, we need to get across the railroad station platform to take another train to Poland. There is barely any room to stand on the platform that is covered with hundreds of people.

We find a Russian lieutenant and ask him to help us. We want him to carry the suitcase, full of shoe leather, from the Czech train to the Polish train. Our thinking is that if the Russian lieutenant carries the suitcase, we will escape the suitcase being opened and searched by a Polish border guard.

But as luck would have it, a Polish official in charge of the border patrol sees the suitcase being handed over to the Russian lieutenant. Because I walk next to the Russian lieutenant, the official assumes the suitcase is mine. He tells me I'm under arrest. I stay calm.

He and I push through the mass of people as he takes me to a small shack-like wooden building to the right of the platform. Inside are a desk and two chairs. I need to show him the document with the triangular stamp. The official points for me to stand in front of the wooden desk. He sits down and moves some papers to the side of his desk. He asks me my name.

"Jozek Lipschutz. It's not my suitcase."

"If it's not your suitcase, then you will not care if the suitcase goes and you stay. Empty your pockets and put the contents on the desk."

I am quiet as he begins to go through my items: identity papers, a small amount of Austrian money, and a document stating

I had previously been to Poland returning from a concentration camp and was not repatriating at this time.

At last, he comes to the triangular stamp. He jumps up from his chair and salutes me. "I'm sorry, I'm sorry," he says over and over again.

With a sense of urgency, he quickly shoves my items on his desk into my hands and rushes me out of the building. We run to the train platform and push through the massive crowd of people. He takes a whistle out of his pocket, blows loudly, and makes signs with his hands for the moving train to stop.

The train is packed. People are standing on steps, holding onto railings. Windows are smashed where passengers have crawled through. The Polish official and I squeeze through the throng and board the train. Standing face to face, he shouts above the noise and calls me a Russian hero. He salutes me and maneuvers off of the train. I am on my way, unfortunately without my friend's suitcase.

After returning from my third trip of travels smuggling merchandise to Krakow, Viktor waits for me. A broad smile creeps across his face. "Hanka came looking for you."

I am stunned. "Here, Hanka was here? Hanka is alive! Where is she?"

"I thought you were still in Krakow. I gave her money to take the train to go back."

"She was in Krakow?"

"She heard from someone who saw you here and came looking for you. Roman, Wilus, and her mother are alive too."

I marvel at my luck. Hanka found me. Hanka, Hanka, is alive. She's alive! Viktor says she's staying with Roman at the Jewish cemetery. Her mother is in the Bergen-Belsen Displaced Persons camp. Her father died after a death march from Auschwitz to Mauthausen and from there to Camp Flossenburg. Wilus is recuperating from a mastoid operation in a Catholic hospital in Warsaw. My love is alive!

I leave the next day with one of our employees. We cross three guarded borders with some delays. I can't wait to see Hanka.

When we meet at the cemetery, she can't stop crying. I have tears of rejoicing too. We went through so much to get to this place, to overcome all the horrific things that were forced upon us. Her tears land on my face as I hug and kiss her. I don't want to let her go. We are full of happiness.

She looks wonderful. Her hair is short, her body thin. Her dark eyes still have the sparkle and spunk of when she first bumped into me at the Podgorze airport labor camp.

Hanka tells me that Lilka, who was her brother Manek's girlfriend, heard Roman on the radio. Roman was testifying against a *kapo* from Auschwitz. Soon after the broadcast, Hanka and Roman were reunited at the cemetery.

They live in Mr. Horowitz's house on the first floor. It's a small building. Before the war, Mr. Horowitz prepared bodies to be buried in the Jewish cemetery. He has a small apartment on the second floor.

I send a guy, six-feet-tall and stocky, who works for Viktor and me and knows his way around, to the hospital in Warsaw to bring Wilus back to us.

Chapter 33

We Need to Get Out of Krakow

Hanka

Jozek is alive! He's alive! My heart is singing. My head is spinning. He is thin but handsome as ever.

He's taking charge of things. He has Wilus brought back to us from the hospital in Warsaw. Wilus looks older than his nine years, more mature. He has put weight on and has bangs on his forehead. His ear is bandaged from the mastoid operation. He doesn't stop talking about the nuns in the hospital wearing their pointed hats. I think of him all alone, of having the operation without parents or family to hold his hands.

My baby brother looks older than twelve. Roman did a good job taking care of Wilus. He kept both of them alive. It's a blessing Lilka heard Roman speaking on the radio.

I had hoped with all my heart that Tatus would survive. Mamusia and I talked about seeing him again. Believing Tatus and the others were alive sustained us.

It's getting very difficult to stay in Krakow. We have witnessed pogroms by Polish people against Jews outside the cemetery. We have seen outbursts of attacks, beatings, and killings. Jozek and I decide we need to get out of Krakow and into the American zone of Austria. He trades all of his German and Polish money into American money.

By now everyone knows Jozek is here. He knows how to cross the borders. Everyone is coming and saying that they want him to take them across the borders. They beg him to take them.

At the beginning, it was easy for everyone to cross the borders. Now it's much harder. Jozek hates to turn people down, but he doesn't see how he can handle them all. Jozek decides seventeen will be a manageable number of people. In addition to himself, me, Roman, Wilus, Viktor and his wife Regina, and the two workers, Jozek chooses nine other people. It's a practical decision on his part.

Chapter 34

It Is an Adventure

Jozek

Someone I have chosen to take with me is a fellow named Zeftel. He was a Jewish policeman, possibly third in command, in Plaszow. He never gave me any problems. But the night before we were to leave Krakow, Russian police arrested him.

A young man had made a charge against Zeftel. It is a complicated story. In Plaszow, Jewish policemen caught prisoners who had no permanent assignments and forced them to go inside a fence enclosure. The prisoners were usually found hiding in their barracks.

The Germans ordered about a hundred people or more to be put into the fenced enclosure in a square about one hundred feet long and six or seven feet wide. This enclosure had one narrow entrance, about two feet wide, and was guarded by a Jewish policeman. At the end of the day, Germans walked the captured prisoners up to the end of the hill and executed them.

Zeftel on his own would find older prisoners in camp and try to make a deal with the Jewish policeman at the gate to exchange them for young prisoners. His belief was, and at the end of the war it proved correct, that a young person had a better chance to survive than an old person. This, to the best of my knowledge, happened every week or two depending upon the number of prisoners the Germans considered essential to fulfill their forced labor requirements.

I knew this was happening when I came to Plaszow from the airport labor camp, and I knew it continued at least until August of 1944. Pretty much everyone in the camp was aware of the situation. I never heard anyone complain about it. I sure didn't. I was one of the young ones.

The young man accused Zeftel of exchanging his grandfather for a young prisoner in the fenced-in square. His complaint to the Russian police was that Zeftel had no right to make decisions as to who would live and who would die. Morally the grandson is probably right, and I understand how he feels. But realistically, Zeftel was trying to keep a Jew alive who had a better chance to survive. It was a balancing act on Zeftel's part.

Zeftel was arrested the night before we were going to leave, and we didn't wait for him.

We start our trip as scheduled the following morning. Walking outside of Krakow, we encounter two women. One of them was Manek's girlfriend, Lilka, who heard Roman on the radio. Hanka urges me to have the two women join our group. I agree to take them.

We are able to cross the Russian-Occupied Czechoslovakian border with my paper. When we want to get out of the Occupied-Czechoslovakia border, we run into trouble. Guards refuse to honor my paper with the stamp. I don't know why. I am faced with having to work out how to get from here to the American-Occupied sector of Austria.

We stay near the border of Budzejowice, a beer-producing town, for two days. There must be a way around this. I have to come up with a plan. Then a train comes to this town with American soldiers bringing Czechoslovakian and Soviet people. The Americans unload the train, and it's going back to Austria.

It's lucky for us that Lilka attended the university before the war and can converse in broken English.

She is bright, an attractive brunette, and very sexy. She manages somehow to convince the Americans we should be allowed to hide in the train.

The Americans tell us to come quietly. We make our way carefully between boxcars with a soldier. There are about sixty cars. We go into one of the empty middle cars, and the American soldier shuts and locks the door. We put blankets out on the floor to sit and sleep on.

The train has to cross over the river. When it comes to the bridge, the train stops. I caution everyone to keep quiet because Russians will be inspecting the train. I stand near the door. I have to handle this right.

There is banging on nearby train doors. Shortly after, there is a bang on our door. The door opens. Two Russian soldiers peek in, see us and enter holding rifles.

I am prepared for them. I call out, "Vodka, Vodka," and shove two bottles and the paper with the triangle at them. They barely examine the paper, but look at the Vodka.

Not wanting to share the Vodka with the other Russian soldiers, one of the Russian soldiers leans out of the car and says to a Russian soldier outside, "He has a pass. He can go."

The two Russian soldiers wait inside with us while they hear the banging on the next door and the soldiers move on to other boxcars. Then they take the two bottles of Vodka from me, step out, lock the door, and walk away.

Thank G-d the bottles of Vodka satisfied them. The flutters in my chest deflate like a flattened pillow. I notice Wilus' eyes wide with excitement. I realize it is an adventure to him. It's an adventure to me too but also serious business. I must take control of anything that comes our way and make sure we have a positive outcome. Everyone's life in this boxcar depends upon me.

As the train moves again, we are in good spirits. Our faces radiate smiles and our talks focus on the future. The past is too painful to discuss. We talk about wanting to get married, build homes, and forget about concentration camps.

I tell Hanka I will do anything and work hard to support us financially. I have limited skills in English. My father didn't believe we should learn the language. He was a Zionist and used to have a tutor come to the house to teach Hebrew to my brothers and me.

We stay in the cramped boxcar for a week before the train crosses the border. We get off of the train on the American side in Austria without difficulty. We walk through a field to enter the American checkpoint. Hanka, Roman, Wilus, and I walk slightly ahead of the group.

Suddenly, an American soldier stands up from his hiding place in the field and points his rifle at us. Adrenaline pumps through my body. I caution the group to stay back with my hand and yell, "Lilka, quick! Come here! Tell him who we are."

In her broken English, she talks to the soldier while he keeps the rifle leveled at us. She explains we are Jewish survivors of the camps on our way to the American sector and have no weapons. Will he believe her and let us go through?

With the rifle in his right hand, he gestures to her to stay where she is while he reaches inside his shirt. With his free hand he pulls out a gold mezuzah on a chain. "Do you know what this is?"

"Mezuzah," she blurts out.

The rest of the group holds their breath while we watch the situation play out. We pass his test. He stops pointing his American M1 dark brown rifle at us and says we can go ahead. Lilka proved valuable again. I'm glad we have her along to speak English.

In a straggly line, with expressions of joy and renewed energy in our steps, we cross the field to safety to the American's checkpoint. Their booth is on one side, and the Russian's booth is on the other side.

We are in the Ebensee, Austria Displaced Persons camp. We are ready to soak in a new way of life.

Chapter 35

1945 to 1948 - I Take the Money

Jozek

The authorities don't know what to do with us, so they put us in displaced persons camps. They do not consider us as a group of Jews, but rather classify us as Polish citizens. I resent this. We were singled out and killed because we were Jews not because we were Polish citizens. Nothing I can do about this. It is what it is.

Hanka becomes more anxious about her mother who is in the Bergen-Belsen Displaced Persons camp in the northwestern part of Germany. The camp, located in the British-Occupation zone, is near the site of the former Bergen-Belsen concentration camp.

The British Army Jewish Brigade Group, fighting under the Zionist flag, was formally established in 1944. Five thousand Jewish volunteers from Palestine were organized into three infantry battalions and several supporting units. This brigade was mostly active in Italy, where they fought against the Germans until the war's end.

Some soldiers from the Jewish Brigade are helping to create displaced persons camps for Jewish survivors. Members of this group were successful in assisting to set up some kind of police force here in the Austria camp. I have joined in with their rallies and marches in support of a Jewish State.

It's the fall of 1945, and the brigade is organizing people wanting to travel in trucks to the Bergen-Belsen Displaced Persons camp. Hanka and I manage to have Roman become part of this group. One of my friends, who is going on the trip, will watch over Hanka's brother. Roman wants to be with his mother in the Bergen-Belsen Displaced Persons camp. He wants to have his Bar Mitzvah there. Roman feels his Bar Mitzvah will honor his father and show that young Jewish boys are survivors. He struggles to be strong but chokes on his words when he talks about his father not being alive to witness his Bar Mitzvah.

Months pass and late in January of 1946, Hanka says she wants to be with her mother and her brother.

We decide to leave the Austria Displaced Persons camp and go to the Bergen-Belsen Displaced Persons camp to live. We take Wilus with us.

Trains do not go all the way through to Bergen-Belsen. We have to find other transportation to complete our trip. We decide to rest in Tirschenreuth, Germany.

We continue north any way we can, by train, wagon, and horse and buggy. It's not easy, and it's not quick. We are confronted with delay after delay. I have to bribe everyone with one-dollar bills in American money.

Eventually in early March after two months, we arrive at the Bergen–Belsen Displaced Persons camp. I have twenty-two American dollars left.

Bergen-Belsen was a German army base during the war. The camp's hospital wards were turned into living quarters. We live in quarters that are like a hotel but not nearly as elegant. Our three rooms are on the second floor but not next to each other. Hanka, her mother, Malia, and brother, Roman, live in one room. Her cousin, Wilus, and I are together in a room. Malia's friend, Irwin Abramowicz, lives in another room.

Once again, I have to turn to the black market in order to support us, but I'm not successful.

One day an elderly gentleman comes up to me and introduces himself as Mr. Koenig. He asks me, "Was your father's name Abraham?"

"Yes. How did you know my father?"

"We were in the same business of selling raw materials to chocolate and candy factories. He was a nice man, well respected by myself and others in our trade."

Mr. Koenig relates that he belonged to our synagogue and chanted payers on the *bimah* with my father. I search my memory but come up empty. I don't remember him.

He is very cordial and says he and his wife would like me to come to dinner that evening. I accept his invitation.

After a pleasant dinner where we recall happier times in Krakow, he tells his wife to go into their bedroom and bring back two packages. She hands him the packages, and he opens them up.

Each package contains fifty thousand German marks. I wonder why he is showing me the money.

He hands me the two packages of German marks and says, "Jozek, take this money and go into business. I have the utmost confidence in you. Your father was a man of principle. I miss him. I know you will return the money when you make a profit."

Without any hesitation, I take the money and thank him. This is quite a surprise. I'll be able to expand my black market business. I shake his hand and tell him I'm honored by his faith in me. I tell him he can count on me to return the money in full.

After shaking hands and thanking his wife for the delicious dinner, I stand outside their building and look up at the night-covered sky. I say out loud, "Thank you Tatus for being so highly respected by your friend."

I know exactly what to do with the loan of the money. I use his money to buy broken gold pieces from several dealers in and around the displaced persons camp. I become acquainted with a jeweler in Cologne, Germany, who takes the pieces and sends them to a smelting company. In a few days, minus his profit, he returns 24-carat bands to me based on the average certification value of the gold I supplied. I sell the 24-carat bands back to the dealers who had originally sold me the gold pieces. The difference in cost between the broken gold pieces and the 24-carat bands is my profit. With my profits, I buy merchandise in Cologne to sell in the displaced persons camp.

People congregate in a plaza in the camp to do business on the black market. It has become a profitable way to sell goods after the war and many people are doing this.

About a year and a half later, I'm able to return the money to Mr. Koenig. He is pleased with my success. He tells me he had faith in me. He talks again of his friendship with my father. He says they were friendly competitors and would help each other out. Lucky for me he has honored my father by doing a good deed for me.

After repaying the loan to Mr. Koenig, I stop dealing in gold pieces and start a new black market venture. I buy a coffee-roasting machine in Cologne with two partners. We sell roasted coffee. Coffee comes into the displaced persons camp, and the head of the camp illegally sells it to my partners and me. I obtain permission to have the coffee-roasting machine installed in an attic.

We sell coffee to Germans, a sack at a time. The roasted coffee reminds me of better times, times when I sat in cafes in Krakow and drank coffee with friends. That's a life long gone.

There's also a larger coffee-roasting black market business in the camp. My two partners and I cut our price to compete with them. They approach my partners and me to sell our business to them. We refuse. Instead we offer them a deal to become partners for a small percentage of the overall profits.

Chapter 36

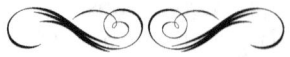

The Wedding Takes Place

Hanka

Jozek and I marry in April of 1948. There is no purpose in waiting. I'm twenty-two-years-old. Whatever the future holds, we will face it together. Our love will carry us through.

The wedding takes place in a canteen dining room. I wear a white silk wedding gown and a long veil made by a dressmaker in Hanover, Germany. Jozek says I look beautiful. He is handsome in his dark suit.

We sign a *Ketubah*, a Jewish marriage contract, before the ceremony. Under the *chuppah*, the wedding canopy, Jozek wears a *kittle*, a white knee-length cotton robe, over his suit, and a *tallis*. I love him with all my heart. I know I will be good for him.

An orthodox rabbi performs the traditional Jewish marriage ceremony. Jozek puts a 14-carat thin gold wedding band on my index finger. The gold band was made for me by a jeweler Jozek once did business with in Cologne, Germany. Jozek does the breaking of the glass by stepping on it and crushing it with his right foot. This commemorates the destruction of the Temple in Jerusalem more than two thousand years ago.

About fifty guests shout, '*Mazel Tov*', congratulations, to us after the breaking of the glass. They hug and kiss us on our cheeks after the ceremony. It's a wonderful happy time to be alive. We have recorded music playing and a buffet for our guests to eat.

How I wish I could dance with my father. Flashing before me is his straightened back and the strength of his hands as we whirl around the dance floor. How I wish my brother Manek was alive to make a toast. It would be sentimental and also funny. He wouldn't let me forget I'm his little sister.

Later our small family retires to Jozek's and my living quarters where we have a quiet meal together. I wish Jozek's parents, sister, and two brothers were alive to see us married. I wish, I wish, I wish but I have to be happy without them.

Chapter 37

We Live Like a Family

Jozek

It goes without saying, I'm extremely happy to be married to Hanka. She is all I have. She's my whole world. I promise myself I will not let anything happen to her. For a quick moment under the *chuppah*, Mamusia, Tatus, Milek, Manek, and Sabcia, appeared in a vision before my eyes. It hurts not having them alongside me on my wedding day.

I look ahead to a good life. That's what we want, all of us survivors, to start anew. A lot of weddings are taking place in the Bergen-Belsen Displaced Persons camp.

Wilus moves out of my room and shares a room with Malia's friend, Mr. Abramowicz. Roman lives with his mother. I pay money under the table to arrange for us to have three rooms next door to each other.

Hanka's mother is religious and observes Shabbos, Friday evening until sundown on Saturday. I respect her wishes and don't travel to do business on those days. I leave for business on Sunday and return on Thursday.

The Bergen-Belsen Displaced Persons camp has one building in the middle of the camp surrounded by several buildings where people live. A bakery, a place to get a bowl of cereal and other food are in the middle building. We stand in line to get two meals a day. Malia is tired of living this way, so I buy a portable kitchen stove for her to do the cooking. There is an icebox in the apartment. Hanka's mother shops for food, and I give her money to accomplish this. Money is not important to us the way it was before the war. Living safe happy lives is what counts.

I give pocket money to Wilus and Roman each week. I hand them each five cents, which equals thirty marks. There is a movie theater in the camp, but you have to pay for it. We live like a family but in a very poor way.

Chapter 38

1945 to 1948 – I Have No One Else

Wilus

Jewish people start Hebrew schools in the displaced persons camp. Roman and I interact with boys and girls. After classes, we join in with students and ride bicycles into the small town. Each day resembles a normal life for me.

School is fun, something new. I am ten-years-old and attending school for the first time. Roman went to school before the war. He is learning a trade, how to be an auto mechanic. We are taught Hebrew and sing songs. I have friends and food to eat. Adults take care of me. I learn to play the accordion. I try out for boxing and am knocked unconscious. I see stars. That's the end of that.

Roman and I play ping-pong and pool around adults. They bet on us and shout out encouragement. It's exciting to hear adults cheering me on. Roman and I win because we are good players. A Hebrew club uses an exercise yard in the middle of four buildings for kids to meet and play games.

Adults play chess outdoors using the ground as a chessboard. They take positions resembling pawns on this made-up chessboard.

I'm okay. I'm happy.

I sit in a truck, knees bent close to my chest, and study cheerful faces of boys and girls from the Hebrew school in the displaced persons camp. Some of them are singing a Hebrew song we learned in class. We are being transported to Hamburg, Germany, on our way to Palestine to help build a Jewish State.

Last night I couldn't sleep. I twisted and turned in bed trying not to wake up Mr. Abramowicz. I didn't have to worry. He snored all night.

I thought about the night when I slept with an unloaded revolver under my pillow. The Jewish Brigade came to school and gave us revolvers to learn how to defend ourselves. We were trained on how to put bullets into the revolver, hold it, and shoot straight. They told us to take the weapon to bed with us and get comfortable handling it. They said the revolver should become a part of us. I liked the feel of the revolver and the power it gave me to defend myself.

I was secretly proud they thought I could handle the gun. It felt good in my hands. The Jewish Brigade collected the guns from us the next day.

I also kept thinking, while I couldn't sleep last night, about how I lived with the constant fear of death in the concentration camps. Today I'm facing a different kind of fear. What happens to me next? For the first time since Goeth murdered my parents in Plaszow, I am safe and content. I experience what it's like to be a normal boy. Hanka, Jozek, Roman, and Aunt Malia, are my family now.

Hanka and Jozek said it would be good for me to go to Palestine with the other orphans. In school they encourage us to go. But no one asked me if I wanted to go, not Hanka, Jozek, Aunt Malia, or even Roman.

I try to hide tears blurring my eyes by resting fingertips on my forehead and hands on my face. I don't want to go to another place. I don't want to start over with other people. Why can't I stay in the displaced persons camp with the family I love and trust?

Early in the morning after hugging and saying goodbye to Jozek and Hanka, I climbed into the truck in the driveway across from the school. I said goodbye to Roman and Aunt Malia last night. They all made it sound as if it was the best thing for me to do, to leave for Palestine. Best thing for whom? Why do they want to get rid of me?

Suddenly, my body takes over. I stand up and maneuver to the edge of the slow moving truck. I jump off and land on my feet. One of the girls calls out my name and asks what I am doing. I don't answer her. I don't look back. I run back to the Bergen-Belsen Displaced Persons camp. I know I'm extra baggage. But so what, I have no one else to go to. I don't have Mamusia and Tatus to care for me. Hanka and Jozek have each other. Roman has his mother. I'm alone.

At the entrance to the camp, I stop running before I walk inside. What will they say to me? Nothing they can do. The truck has left.

When we lived in the Austria Displaced Persons camp, an American Jewish soldier spent time with the family. He wanted to adopt me and take me with him to America. Hanka told the soldier that I needed to remain with my family. Why doesn't she say that now instead of sending me off to Palestine? The American soldier was nice to me.

In the Austria Displaced Persons camp, Viktor's wife, Regina, would hug me and tell me how glad she was I am alive. I liked spending time with her too.

All I want is to be with my family. I rush to their building. When I reach Hanka's and Jozek's room, I take a deep breath before knocking on their door. When Hanka opens the door. She looks at me alarmed.

I talk fast. "I jumped off the truck. I don't want to go to Palestine."

"What happened? Are you all right?" She takes my hand and brings me into the room.

"Wilus, what are you doing here?" Jozek asks me. He's surprised, maybe even shocked.

"I'm not going to Palestine. I'm staying here."

"Don't you want to be with the other children and help build a Jewish State?"

"No. I don't want to leave. I want to be with you and Hanka, Roman, and Aunt Malia."

"If that is what you want, of course you can stay with us." Hanka says and looks to Jozek for confirmation. He shakes his head in agreement. He has no choice. Maybe he'll realize they were wrong to send me away.

"Nobody asked if I wanted to go," I snap.

"It's settled. You don't have to go," Hanka says. She gives me a big hug.

After my parents were murdered, I moved along with everyone else and felt like I belonged to Roman and his mother, to Hanka and Jozek, and also to Uncle Leon, before he was killed. I never considered who would take care of me. I just thought I would be with them. I thought they included me in their family.

I keep my fears hidden. I'm determined no one will see me cry. I try to be helpful and no trouble to anyone. I'll try even harder.

I don't want to start my life over in Palestine with the other orphans. I'm trying to block out thoughts of my parents being murdered. I want to stop remembering getting up in the dark shadows of the morning and seeing a dead body. I don't want to think about the sounds of gunshots and screams at night. I want to forget running with Roman and escaping from Auschwitz. My whole life has been one big concentration camp.

Chapter 39

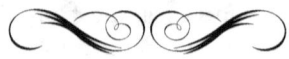

1948 to 1949 – Everything Is Temporary

Jozek

Hanka and I listened to her mother. Malia felt Wilus would be better off in Palestine with the other orphans. She believed he would be looked after there. The Hebrew school in Bergen-Belsen promotes the premise that orphans are needed to help build a Jewish State.

So Wilus wants to be with us, okay, we'll manage. It's just that everything is temporary. We need to determine what to do next. We live in the displaced persons camp for now but it will not be for long. Bergen-Belsen will eventually be shut down. The question becomes where to go.

Hanka, her mother, and I agree we do not want to stay in Germany. France and England are not accepting many people. Poland is out of the question. Once we were proud to be Polish but not anymore. We decide to sign up for immigration to the United States. They say America is a land of opportunity, streets paved in gold.

In 1949, we move to a transit camp, Celle, outside Bremen, Germany, until we can emigrate to the United States.

We are blessed with a daughter, Rosalie, born in Celle in September of 1949. We name her after my mother, Rosalia. She is a pretty baby with hazel eyes and dark brown hair, like her mother's. Life is good.

Wilus is very protective of Rosalie and stays close to her. Once he chased away the German nurse we hired with money I had saved from my black market activities.

Wilus raised his hand at the nurse and yelled, 'Out!' when she wanted to pick up our daughter. I explained to him the nurse is a good German and here to take care of our baby. He still watches and lingers near our daughter.

Malia and Roman receive their visas through relatives, the Goldfarbs, who own a bakery in Brooklyn, New York. Malia and Roman arrive in New York City on Columbus Day 1949. They traveled to America by ship to Boston and then by train to a hotel in New York City.

We're lucky. We get priority treatment because of our baby. Instead of going by ship, we fly to the United States. Others who went by ship made the trip in ten days under very bad conditions.

On the plane, we use a basket covered with white muslin, especially designed for attachment to the seat, in place of a tray table for our daughter. Hanka and I have expectations of a good life ahead.

Chapter 40

I Am the Only Kid

Wilus

We are flying on Scandinavian airlines from Bremen, Germany. Men, women, and babies are passengers on the plane. I am the only kid. I am used to that, being an only kid.

The stewardess takes me into the cockpit where the pilot goes over the controls with me. Back in my seat, I catch parts of the grownups' conversations. They say America's streets are lined with gold.

One place is as good as another. I have no Mamusia and Tatus to take care of me. I'm holding tight onto the only family I have in Hanka, Jozek, and Rosalie, and Aunt Malia and Roman.

The family originally thought I would go to America with Aunt Malia and Roman and live with them.

I'm okay with that. They put Hanka's maiden name Ferber after my name. But I don't have a visa from the Goldfarbs like Roman and his mother.

That's why I'm going to America with Hanka, Jozek, and Rosalie. It's good Rosalie is sleeping. The flight stops at Glasgow and goes on to Newfoundland. We eventually come to the Newark, New Jersey airport. The flight takes us eighteen hours. We arrive in New York City on December 21, 1949.

Chapter 41

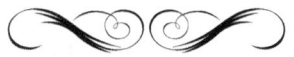

We Come to Philadelphia

Jozek

I hope to earn enough money to support the four of us. We stay in a hotel on Broadway in New York City, New York. Hanka and Wilus take turns rocking our daughter to sleep in our room so she will not cry and wake up others in the hotel. She sleeps in the bottom drawer of a chest.

Our documents finally come from the Philadelphia Jewish Family Service, one of the Jewish relief organizations. After three weeks under the aegis of the Jewish organization, we come to Philadelphia, Pennsylvania. We are given an apartment, one room and a kitchen, on Jackson Street, a side street off of Snyder Avenue in South Philadelphia.

I had learned some English in Germany and am given a job at the Jewish Family Service for one dollar an hour. At this you cannot earn a living. I have some American money I converted from marks that I earned from my black market dealings. We have a very hard time making ends meet. The organization eventually finds me a job with a furrier on Walnut Street where I earn forty dollars a week.

A couple of weeks later, we need to move out for another family. We are on our own. Luckily with my salary I am able to afford another apartment. We slowly start to return to a kind of normal life.

I feel I did the best I could with the cards I was dealt. I took risks because I willed myself to survive. I still question where G-d was when the Germans murdered my family and all those innocent people. I'm bitter. I was brought up in a religious and caring home. My father would change his money into rolls of zloty coins and carry it in his pockets during the week. He would give coins to beggars.

Looking back, my life of love and death started with a wonderful family: Tatus, Mamusia, Milek, Manek, and Sabcia. They're all gone. I escaped from the shadows of death, shackled to the past with horrific memories of lives tortured and lost. It's hard for me to let go of my hate.

I must now start afresh, laying down roots for a new life, in a new land, with Hanka and our baby daughter, Rosalie, and Wilus.

Austria Displaced Persons Camp

Left:
Hanka Ferber and Lilka (last name unknown)

Right:
Wilus Schnitzer (center) and friends

Above:
American soldier (name unknown), Viktor Lewis, Regina Lewis, Wilus Schnitzer, Jozek Lipschutz, and friends

Left:
Viktor and Regina Lewis

Bergen-Belsen Displaced Persons Camp

Hanka Ferber and Jozek Lipschutz on their wedding day

Wilus Schnitzer and Regina Lewis

From left: Wilus Schnitzer, Hanka Ferber Lipschutz, Roman Ferber, and friends at Hanka and Jozek Lipschutz's wedding

Miriam Segal Shnycer

Wilus Schnitzer (last row, second from left) attends school

Jozek Lipschutz marches in support of Palestine

Adults used as pieces in a chess game

Epilogue

Joseph Lipshutz (Jozek Lipschutz) was hired in 1953 as a tester in the laboratory of Schaevitz Engineering, Pennsauken, New Jersey. He studied electrical engineering at Drexel Institute of Technology, Philadelphia, Pennsylvania at night. In 1971, he became vice president of Operations at Schaevitz Engineering.

The design for the fingers of the presidents' hands at the Presidents Hall at Disney was the result of one of several patents he held for Schaevitz Engineering. There were two patents for the space shuttle, which were never used.

He continued to wrestle with the moral dilemma of exchanging an older prisoner for a younger prisoner in Plaszow.

He destroyed the triangular stamp soon after coming to the United States because of the prevalent fear of Communism during the McCarthy era.

Ann Lipshutz (Hanka Ferber Lipschutz) and Joseph had another daughter, Lynn, born in Philadelphia, Pennsylvania. Ann always kept family and friends close. She remained a warm loving person taking pleasure in performing charity work.

Ann and Joseph Lipshutz remained in Philadelphia, Pennsylvania.

Ann Lipshutz died in 1966.

Joseph Lipshutz married Doris Little in 1968. He retired from Schaevitz Engineering in 1980, and they moved to Fort Myers, Florida. He lectured on his experiences during the Holocaust.

Together their merged family has four children, nine grandchildren, and twelve great grandchildren.

Joseph Lipshutz died in 2012.

Doris Lipshutz died in 2017.

Malia Ferber married Irvin Abramowicz, her friend from the Bergen-Belsen Displaced Persons camp. Roman lived with them in Bronx, New York. She took pride in her matchmaking skills. She helped care for Hanka as her daughter struggled with cancer.

Malia Ferber died in 1987.

Roman Ferber earned a bachelor degree from Hunter College in 1958, followed by a master's degree and a Ph.D. degree from New York University. He served in the army and was a Korean War veteran. He held key urban planning and economic development positions under several New York mayoral administrations and performed consulting work after retiring in 2002.

He spoke about the Holocaust and visited Poland several times. His book, *Journey of Ashes, A Boyhood in the Holocaust*, is co-authored with Anna Ray-Jones.

He married Maxine Singer. They lived in Monroe County, New Jersey. They have three children and five grandchildren.

Roman Ferber died in 2016.

William Shnycer (Wilus Schnitzer) lived with Ann and Joseph Lipshutz after coming to the United States. He began his schooling studying the English language for a year and starting public school in the ninth grade. He graduated with an accounting degree from Pierce College, Philadelphia, Pennsylvania. Before serving in the Army Reserves, he married the book's author, Miriam Segal.

In 1963, he began his professional career as an accountant with AAMCO Transmissions Inc. He advanced up the chain of command to president and chief operations officer and then to vice chairman. Upon his retirement, he acted as a consultant to the company until its sale in 2006.

He and his wife have two children and four grandchildren. They reside in Villanova, Pennsylvania, a suburb of Philadelphia.

Roman and Wilus were proud to act on the option of serving in the United States Army. They wanted to do their part in contributing to their new country.

Rosalie Lipshutz was married wearing her mother's wedding ring.

Five people from these three intertwined families, consisting of fourteen members, survived the Holocaust. Despite all the inhuman suffering they endured, and against all odds, they became part of America's success stories. Their determination, courage, and luck led to their achievements. They discovered the American dream, embraced it, nourished it, and molded it to fit their lives.

Acknowledgments

I have a wealth of people to acknowledge for helping, supporting, and encouraging me on the way to making *Of Love and Death* a reality.

Heartfelt thanks to my sister-in-law, Rosalie Swartz, daughter of Holocaust survivors, Ann and Joseph Lipshutz, who read drafts, bounced ideas around with me, and shared insights into the characters' lives.

My thanks to Thomas Keneally for his book, *Schindler's List* and to Steven Spielberg for his movie on Keneally's book. The book and the movie opened the door for my husband and others to speak about their lives during the Holocaust.

Elinor J. Brecher's book, *Schindler's Legacy*, has true stories of survivors. Some of the characters in my book have been profiled in hers.

I owe a debt of gratitude to Dr. Shrikrishna (Krish) Singh, publisher of Auctus Publishers, for his enthusiasm in publishing my book. For this first-time author, he made the process a pleasant and smooth experience. Thanks to Rich Bank for helping to bring my book to fruition by sending the manuscript to Krish and for his editorial advice and support. Sincere thanks to Sarah Eldridge for the book design and to Angela De Vecchio for her cover art and illustration. They beautifully captured the spirit of my book.

Longtime friend, Marilyn Roberts, has made me a better writer. Many a Monday morning was spent talking on the phone, computers clicking, going over aspects of the book. Much thanks to Marilyn for her skillfully copyediting the book.

Heartfelt thanks to Catherine DePino who critiqued a draft, advised me many times during my writing process, and encouraged me to have my story published.

My sisters, Roslyn Gorin and Bernice Greenstein, were helpful in discussing the characters, reading drafts, and giving me feedback. Roslyn, also, has my deep appreciation for assisting me in the copyediting process. Reading books have been a big part of our lives and a joy instilled in us by our parents, Esther and Abraham Segal. As children, our mother took us most Sundays by bus to the main branch of the Free Library of Philadelphia. Our father was constantly reading books and Jewish newspapers.

My thanks to Jim Heubach, whose viewpoints on my draft were invaluable to me since he doesn't know any of the people involved and could provide a fresh perspective.

Sadly, Jim Clark, captain of the weekly Writers' C(r)amp group, passed away last year. Jim gave excellent critiques and was a supporter of my story. Carol Sabik-Jaffe was a member of the group and has offered me ongoing insightful suggestions.

I would be remiss if I didn't give boundless thanks to my family and friends who have been enthusiastic cheerleaders and have relentlessly supported and encouraged me to get my book out there. They are too long to list but are forever in my heart.

I'm blessed with wonderful daughters and sons-in-law, Abby and Steve Golberg and Hillary and Lewis Silver, and grandchildren, Eric and Cara Golberg and Ethan and Lindsey Silver. They were my sounding boards, read drafts, and gave me their opinions. A special thanks goes to Hillary for her professional advice and assistance.

Lastly but foremost is my husband, Will, who courageously delved into the horrors of his childhood, read drafts, and was always there for me. Will is the love of my life, my inspiration, my hero. He completes me.

About the Author

Miriam Segal Shnycer is a journalist and freelance writer. She has written numerous magazine and newspaper articles. She has worked as an editor of several magazines for NAPCO Media (formerly North American Publishing Company), Philadelphia, Pennsylvania. She is a longtime member of the Board of Directors of the Philadelphia Writers' Conference. She received her BA from Temple University, School of Communications and Theater (now School of Media and Communication). She is a member of Kappa Tau Alpha, the journalism honor fraternity. Of *Love and Death: Young Holocaust Survivors' Passage to Freedom* is her first book. She and her husband, William, live in Villanova, a suburb of Philadelphia.

www.ingramcontent.com/pod-product-compliance
Lightning Source LLC
Chambersburg PA
CBHW052028070526
44584CB00016B/1957